C-4714   CAREER EXAMINATION SERIES

This is your
PASSBOOK for...

Storeroom Supervisor

Test Preparation Study Guide
Questions & Answers

COPYRIGHT NOTICE

This book is SOLELY intended for, is sold ONLY to, and its use is RESTRICTED to individual, bona fide applicants or candidates who qualify by virtue of having seriously filed applications for appropriate license, certificate, professional and/or promotional advancement, higher school matriculation, scholarship, or other legitimate requirements of education and/or governmental authorities.

This book is NOT intended for use, class instruction, tutoring, training, duplication, copying, reprinting, excerption, or adaptation, etc., by:

1) Other publishers
2) Proprietors and/or Instructors of "Coaching" and/or Preparatory Courses
3) Personnel and/or Training Divisions of commercial, industrial, and governmental organizations
4) Schools, colleges, or universities and/or their departments and staffs, including teachers and other personnel
5) Testing Agencies or Bureaus
6) Study groups which seek by the purchase of a single volume to copy and/or duplicate and/or adapt this material for use by the group as a whole without having purchased individual volumes for each of the members of the group
7) Et al.

Such persons would be in violation of appropriate Federal and State statutes.

PROVISION OF LICENSING AGREEMENTS – Recognized educational, commercial, industrial, and governmental institutions and organizations, and others legitimately engaged in educational pursuits, including training, testing, and measurement activities, may address request for a licensing agreement to the copyright owners, who will determine whether, and under what conditions, including fees and charges, the materials in this book may be used them. In other words, a licensing facility exists for the legitimate use of the material in this book on other than an individual basis. However, it is asseverated and affirmed here that the material in this book CANNOT be used without the receipt of the express permission of such a licensing agreement from the Publishers. Inquiries re licensing should be addressed to the company, attention rights and permissions department.

All rights reserved, including the right of reproduction in whole or in part, in any form or by any means, electronic or mechanical, including photocopying, recording, or by any information storage and retrieval system, without permission in writing from the Publisher.

Copyright © 2025 by
National Learning Corporation

212 Michael Drive, Syosset, NY 11791
(516) 921-8888 • www.passbooks.com
E-mail: info@passbooks.com

PASSBOOK® SERIES

THE *PASSBOOK® SERIES* has been created to prepare applicants and candidates for the ultimate academic battlefield – the examination room.

At some time in our lives, each and every one of us may be required to take an examination – for validation, matriculation, admission, qualification, registration, certification, or licensure.

Based on the assumption that every applicant or candidate has met the basic formal educational standards, has taken the required number of courses, and read the necessary texts, the *PASSBOOK® SERIES* furnishes the one special preparation which may assure passing with confidence, instead of failing with insecurity. Examination questions – together with answers – are furnished as the basic vehicle for study so that the mysteries of the examination and its compounding difficulties may be eliminated or diminished by a sure method.

This book is meant to help you pass your examination provided that you qualify and are serious in your objective.

The entire field is reviewed through the huge store of content information which is succinctly presented through a provocative and challenging approach – the question-and-answer method.

A climate of success is established by furnishing the correct answers at the end of each test.

You soon learn to recognize types of questions, forms of questions, and patterns of questioning. You may even begin to anticipate expected outcomes.

You perceive that many questions are repeated or adapted so that you can gain acute insights, which may enable you to score many sure points.

You learn how to confront new questions, or types of questions, and to attack them confidently and work out the correct answers.

You note objectives and emphases, and recognize pitfalls and dangers, so that you may make positive educational adjustments.

Moreover, you are kept fully informed in relation to new concepts, methods, practices, and directions in the field.

You discover that you are actually taking the examination all the time: you are preparing for the examination by "taking" an examination, not by reading extraneous and/or supererogatory textbooks.

In short, this PASSBOOK®, used directedly, should be an important factor in helping you to pass your test.

STOREROOM SUPERVISOR

DUTIES:
   Storeroom Supervisors perform supervisory work at varying degrees of difficulty and responsibility involving the receipt, checking, classification, storage, distribution, and issuance of materials and supplies. They supervise employees engaged in the loading and unloading of trucks, unpacking, counting, sorting, marking, verifying, and placing of materials and supplies received on pallets, shelves, and in bins, filling of requisitions, and in taking inventory; identify and handle obsolete materials, weigh scrap, make payments of freight charges, conduct research and provide data associated with the processing of disbursements; prepare reports and keep records; operate computers and perform functions related to updating the inventory management systems; drive motor vehicles; and perform related work.

SCOPE OF THE EXAMINATION:
   The written test is designed to test for knowledge, skills, and/or abilities as follows: Knowledge of the procedures related to the receipt, storage, issuance and transporting of stock; record-keeping and inventory-control techniques; including the use of computer systems such as for the updating, storage, and retrieval of information; supervisory methods and techniques; safe work practices and procedures; job-related mathematical computations.

HOW TO TAKE A TEST

I. YOU MUST PASS AN EXAMINATION

A. WHAT EVERY CANDIDATE SHOULD KNOW

Examination applicants often ask us for help in preparing for the written test. What can I study in advance? What kinds of questions will be asked? How will the test be given? How will the papers be graded?

As an applicant for a civil service examination, you may be wondering about some of these things. Our purpose here is to suggest effective methods of advance study and to describe civil service examinations.

Your chances for success on this examination can be increased if you know how to prepare. Those "pre-examination jitters" can be reduced if you know what to expect. You can even experience an adventure in good citizenship if you know why civil service exams are given.

B. WHY ARE CIVIL SERVICE EXAMINATIONS GIVEN?

Civil service examinations are important to you in two ways. As a citizen, you want public jobs filled by employees who know how to do their work. As a job seeker, you want a fair chance to compete for that job on an equal footing with other candidates. The best-known means of accomplishing this two-fold goal is the competitive examination.

Exams are widely publicized throughout the nation. They may be administered for jobs in federal, state, city, municipal, town or village governments or agencies.

Any citizen may apply, with some limitations, such as the age or residence of applicants. Your experience and education may be reviewed to see whether you meet the requirements for the particular examination. When these requirements exist, they are reasonable and applied consistently to all applicants. Thus, a competitive examination may cause you some uneasiness now, but it is your privilege and safeguard.

C. HOW ARE CIVIL SERVICE EXAMS DEVELOPED?

Examinations are carefully written by trained technicians who are specialists in the field known as "psychological measurement," in consultation with recognized authorities in the field of work that the test will cover. These experts recommend the subject matter areas or skills to be tested; only those knowledges or skills important to your success on the job are included. The most reliable books and source materials available are used as references. Together, the experts and technicians judge the difficulty level of the questions.

Test technicians know how to phrase questions so that the problem is clearly stated. Their ethics do not permit "trick" or "catch" questions. Questions may have been tried out on sample groups, or subjected to statistical analysis, to determine their usefulness.

Written tests are often used in combination with performance tests, ratings of training and experience, and oral interviews. All of these measures combine to form the best-known means of finding the right person for the right job.

II. HOW TO PASS THE WRITTEN TEST

A. NATURE OF THE EXAMINATION

To prepare intelligently for civil service examinations, you should know how they differ from school examinations you have taken. In school you were assigned certain definite pages to read or subjects to cover. The examination questions were quite detailed and usually emphasized memory. Civil service exams, on the other hand, try to discover your present ability to perform the duties of a position, plus your potentiality to learn these duties. In other words, a civil service exam attempts to predict how successful you will be. Questions cover such a broad area that they cannot be as minute and detailed as school exam questions.

In the public service similar kinds of work, or positions, are grouped together in one "class." This process is known as *position-classification*. All the positions in a class are paid according to the salary range for that class. One class title covers all of these positions, and they are all tested by the same examination.

B. FOUR BASIC STEPS

1) Study the announcement

How, then, can you know what subjects to study? Our best answer is: "Learn as much as possible about the class of positions for which you've applied." The exam will test the knowledge, skills and abilities needed to do the work.

Your most valuable source of information about the position you want is the official exam announcement. This announcement lists the training and experience qualifications. Check these standards and apply only if you come reasonably close to meeting them.

The brief description of the position in the examination announcement offers some clues to the subjects which will be tested. Think about the job itself. Review the duties in your mind. Can you perform them, or are there some in which you are rusty? Fill in the blank spots in your preparation.

Many jurisdictions preview the written test in the exam announcement by including a section called "Knowledge and Abilities Required," "Scope of the Examination," or some similar heading. Here you will find out specifically what fields will be tested.

2) Review your own background

Once you learn in general what the position is all about, and what you need to know to do the work, ask yourself which subjects you already know fairly well and which need improvement. You may wonder whether to concentrate on improving your strong areas or on building some background in your fields of weakness. When the announcement has specified "some knowledge" or "considerable knowledge," or has used adjectives like "beginning principles of…" or "advanced … methods," you can get a clue as to the number and difficulty of questions to be asked in any given field. More questions, and hence broader coverage, would be included for those subjects which are more important in the work. Now weigh your strengths and weaknesses against the job requirements and prepare accordingly.

3) Determine the level of the position

Another way to tell how intensively you should prepare is to understand the level of the job for which you are applying. Is it the entering level? In other words, is this the position in which beginners in a field of work are hired? Or is it an intermediate or advanced level? Sometimes this is indicated by such words as "Junior" or "Senior" in the class title. Other jurisdictions use Roman numerals to designate the level – Clerk I, Clerk II, for example. The word "Supervisor" sometimes appears in the title. If the level is not indicated by the title, check the description of duties. Will you be working under very close supervision, or will you have responsibility for independent decisions in this work?

4) Choose appropriate study materials

Now that you know the subjects to be examined and the relative amount of each subject to be covered, you can choose suitable study materials. For beginning level jobs, or even advanced ones, if you have a pronounced weakness in some aspect of your training, read a modern, standard textbook in that field. Be sure it is up to date and has general coverage. Such books are normally available at your library, and the librarian will be glad to help you locate one. For entry-level positions, questions of appropriate difficulty are chosen – neither highly advanced questions, nor those too simple. Such questions require careful thought but not advanced training.

If the position for which you are applying is technical or advanced, you will read more advanced, specialized material. If you are already familiar with the basic principles of your field, elementary textbooks would waste your time. Concentrate on advanced textbooks and technical periodicals. Think through the concepts and review difficult problems in your field.

These are all general sources. You can get more ideas on your own initiative, following these leads. For example, training manuals and publications of the government agency which employs workers in your field can be useful, particularly for technical and professional positions. A letter or visit to the government department involved may result in more specific study suggestions, and certainly will provide you with a more definite idea of the exact nature of the position you are seeking.

III. KINDS OF TESTS

Tests are used for purposes other than measuring knowledge and ability to perform specified duties. For some positions, it is equally important to test ability to make adjustments to new situations or to profit from training. In others, basic mental abilities not dependent on information are essential. Questions which test these things may not appear as pertinent to the duties of the position as those which test for knowledge and information. Yet they are often highly important parts of a fair examination. For very general questions, it is almost impossible to help you direct your study efforts. What we can do is to point out some of the more common of these general abilities needed in public service positions and describe some typical questions.

1) General information

Broad, general information has been found useful for predicting job success in some kinds of work. This is tested in a variety of ways, from vocabulary lists to questions about current events. Basic background in some field of work, such as sociology or economics, may be sampled in a group of questions. Often these are principles which have become familiar to most persons through exposure rather than through formal training. It is difficult to advise you how to study for these questions; being alert to the world around you is our best suggestion.

2) Verbal ability

An example of an ability needed in many positions is verbal or language ability. Verbal ability is, in brief, the ability to use and understand words. Vocabulary and grammar tests are typical measures of this ability. Reading comprehension or paragraph interpretation questions are common in many kinds of civil service tests. You are given a paragraph of written material and asked to find its central meaning.

3) Numerical ability

Number skills can be tested by the familiar arithmetic problem, by checking paired lists of numbers to see which are alike and which are different, or by interpreting charts and graphs. In the latter test, a graph may be printed in the test booklet which you are asked to use as the basis for answering questions.

4) Observation

A popular test for law-enforcement positions is the observation test. A picture is shown to you for several minutes, then taken away. Questions about the picture test your ability to observe both details and larger elements.

5) Following directions

In many positions in the public service, the employee must be able to carry out written instructions dependably and accurately. You may be given a chart with several columns, each column listing a variety of information. The questions require you to carry out directions involving the information given in the chart.

6) Skills and aptitudes

Performance tests effectively measure some manual skills and aptitudes. When the skill is one in which you are trained, such as typing or shorthand, you can practice. These tests are often very much like those given in business school or high school courses. For many of the other skills and aptitudes, however, no short-time preparation can be made. Skills and abilities natural to you or that you have developed throughout your lifetime are being tested.

Many of the general questions just described provide all the data needed to answer the questions and ask you to use your reasoning ability to find the answers. Your best preparation for these tests, as well as for tests of facts and ideas, is to be at your physical and mental best. You, no doubt, have your own methods of getting into an exam-taking mood and keeping "in shape." The next section lists some ideas on this subject.

IV. KINDS OF QUESTIONS

Only rarely is the "essay" question, which you answer in narrative form, used in civil service tests. Civil service tests are usually of the short-answer type. Full instructions for answering these questions will be given to you at the examination. But in case this is your first experience with short-answer questions and separate answer sheets, here is what you need to know:

1) **Multiple-choice Questions**

Most popular of the short-answer questions is the "multiple choice" or "best answer" question. It can be used, for example, to test for factual knowledge, ability to solve problems or judgment in meeting situations found at work.

A multiple-choice question is normally one of three types—
- It can begin with an incomplete statement followed by several possible endings. You are to find the one ending which *best* completes the statement, although some of the others may not be entirely wrong.
- It can also be a complete statement in the form of a question which is answered by choosing one of the statements listed.

- It can be in the form of a problem – again you select the best answer.

Here is an example of a multiple-choice question with a discussion which should give you some clues as to the method for choosing the right answer:

When an employee has a complaint about his assignment, the action which will *best* help him overcome his difficulty is to
    A. discuss his difficulty with his coworkers
    B. take the problem to the head of the organization
    C. take the problem to the person who gave him the assignment
    D. say nothing to anyone about his complaint

In answering this question, you should study each of the choices to find which is best. Consider choice "A" – Certainly an employee may discuss his complaint with fellow employees, but no change or improvement can result, and the complaint remains unresolved. Choice "B" is a poor choice since the head of the organization probably does not know what assignment you have been given, and taking your problem to him is known as "going over the head" of the supervisor. The supervisor, or person who made the assignment, is the person who can clarify it or correct any injustice. Choice "C" is, therefore, correct. To say nothing, as in choice "D," is unwise. Supervisors have and interest in knowing the problems employees are facing, and the employee is seeking a solution to his problem.

2) True/False Questions

The "true/false" or "right/wrong" form of question is sometimes used. Here a complete statement is given. Your job is to decide whether the statement is right or wrong.

SAMPLE: A roaming cell-phone call to a nearby city costs less than a non-roaming call to a distant city.

This statement is wrong, or false, since roaming calls are more expensive.

This is not a complete list of all possible question forms, although most of the others are variations of these common types. You will always get complete directions for answering questions. Be sure you understand *how* to mark your answers – ask questions until you do.

V. RECORDING YOUR ANSWERS

Computer terminals are used more and more today for many different kinds of exams.

For an examination with very few applicants, you may be told to record your answers in the test booklet itself. Separate answer sheets are much more common. If this separate answer sheet is to be scored by machine – and this is often the case – it is highly important that you mark your answers correctly in order to get credit.

An electronic scoring machine is often used in civil service offices because of the speed with which papers can be scored. Machine-scored answer sheets must be marked with a pencil, which will be given to you. This pencil has a high graphite content which responds to the electronic scoring machine. As a matter of fact, stray dots may register as answers, so do not let your pencil rest on the answer sheet while you are pondering the correct answer. Also, if your pencil lead breaks or is otherwise defective, ask for another.

Since the answer sheet will be dropped in a slot in the scoring machine, be careful not to bend the corners or get the paper crumpled.

The answer sheet normally has five vertical columns of numbers, with 30 numbers to a column. These numbers correspond to the question numbers in your test booklet. After each number, going across the page are four or five pairs of dotted lines. These short dotted lines have small letters or numbers above them. The first two pairs may also have a "T" or "F" above the letters. This indicates that the first two pairs only are to be used if the questions are of the true-false type. If the questions are multiple choice, disregard the "T" and "F" and pay attention only to the small letters or numbers.

Answer your questions in the manner of the sample that follows:

32. The largest city in the United States is
    A. Washington, D.C.
    B. New York City
    C. Chicago
    D. Detroit
    E. San Francisco

1) Choose the answer you think is best. (New York City is the largest, so "B" is correct.)
2) Find the row of dotted lines numbered the same as the question you are answering. (Find row number 32)
3) Find the pair of dotted lines corresponding to the answer. (Find the pair of lines under the mark "B.")
4) Make a solid black mark between the dotted lines.

VI. BEFORE THE TEST

Common sense will help you find procedures to follow to get ready for an examination. Too many of us, however, overlook these sensible measures. Indeed, nervousness and fatigue have been found to be the most serious reasons why applicants fail to do their best on civil service tests. Here is a list of reminders:

- Begin your preparation early – Don't wait until the last minute to go scurrying around for books and materials or to find out what the position is all about.
- Prepare continuously – An hour a night for a week is better than an all-night cram session. This has been definitely established. What is more, a night a week for a month will return better dividends than crowding your study into a shorter period of time.
- Locate the place of the exam – You have been sent a notice telling you when and where to report for the examination. If the location is in a different town or otherwise unfamiliar to you, it would be well to inquire the best route and learn something about the building.
- Relax the night before the test – Allow your mind to rest. Do not study at all that night. Plan some mild recreation or diversion; then go to bed early and get a good night's sleep.
- Get up early enough to make a leisurely trip to the place for the test – This way unforeseen events, traffic snarls, unfamiliar buildings, etc. will not upset you.
- Dress comfortably – A written test is not a fashion show. You will be known by number and not by name, so wear something comfortable.

- Leave excess paraphernalia at home – Shopping bags and odd bundles will get in your way. You need bring only the items mentioned in the official notice you received; usually everything you need is provided. Do not bring reference books to the exam. They will only confuse those last minutes and be taken away from you when in the test room.
- Arrive somewhat ahead of time – If because of transportation schedules you must get there very early, bring a newspaper or magazine to take your mind off yourself while waiting.
- Locate the examination room – When you have found the proper room, you will be directed to the seat or part of the room where you will sit. Sometimes you are given a sheet of instructions to read while you are waiting. Do not fill out any forms until you are told to do so; just read them and be prepared.
- Relax and prepare to listen to the instructions
- If you have any physical problem that may keep you from doing your best, be sure to tell the test administrator. If you are sick or in poor health, you really cannot do your best on the exam. You can come back and take the test some other time.

VII. AT THE TEST

The day of the test is here and you have the test booklet in your hand. The temptation to get going is very strong. Caution! There is more to success than knowing the right answers. You must know how to identify your papers and understand variations in the type of short-answer question used in this particular examination. Follow these suggestions for maximum results from your efforts:

1) Cooperate with the monitor

The test administrator has a duty to create a situation in which you can be as much at ease as possible. He will give instructions, tell you when to begin, check to see that you are marking your answer sheet correctly, and so on. He is not there to guard you, although he will see that your competitors do not take unfair advantage. He wants to help you do your best.

2) Listen to all instructions

Don't jump the gun! Wait until you understand all directions. In most civil service tests you get more time than you need to answer the questions. So don't be in a hurry. Read each word of instructions until you clearly understand the meaning. Study the examples, listen to all announcements and follow directions. Ask questions if you do not understand what to do.

3) Identify your papers

Civil service exams are usually identified by number only. You will be assigned a number; you must not put your name on your test papers. Be sure to copy your number correctly. Since more than one exam may be given, copy your exact examination title.

4) Plan your time

Unless you are told that a test is a "speed" or "rate of work" test, speed itself is usually not important. Time enough to answer all the questions will be provided, but this does not mean that you have all day. An overall time limit has been set. Divide the total time (in minutes) by the number of questions to determine the approximate time you have for each question.

5) Do not linger over difficult questions

If you come across a difficult question, mark it with a paper clip (useful to have along) and come back to it when you have been through the booklet. One caution if you do this – be sure to skip a number on your answer sheet as well. Check often to be sure that you have not lost your place and that you are marking in the row numbered the same as the question you are answering.

6) Read the questions

Be sure you know what the question asks! Many capable people are unsuccessful because they failed to *read* the questions correctly.

7) Answer all questions

Unless you have been instructed that a penalty will be deducted for incorrect answers, it is better to guess than to omit a question.

8) Speed tests

It is often better NOT to guess on speed tests. It has been found that on timed tests people are tempted to spend the last few seconds before time is called in marking answers at random – without even reading them – in the hope of picking up a few extra points. To discourage this practice, the instructions may warn you that your score will be "corrected" for guessing. That is, a penalty will be applied. The incorrect answers will be deducted from the correct ones, or some other penalty formula will be used.

9) Review your answers

If you finish before time is called, go back to the questions you guessed or omitted to give them further thought. Review other answers if you have time.

10) Return your test materials

If you are ready to leave before others have finished or time is called, take ALL your materials to the monitor and leave quietly. Never take any test material with you. The monitor can discover whose papers are not complete, and taking a test booklet may be grounds for disqualification.

VIII. EXAMINATION TECHNIQUES

1) Read the general instructions carefully. These are usually printed on the first page of the exam booklet. As a rule, these instructions refer to the timing of the examination; the fact that you should not start work until the signal and must stop work at a signal, etc. If there are any *special* instructions, such as a choice of questions to be answered, make sure that you note this instruction carefully.

2) When you are ready to start work on the examination, that is as soon as the signal has been given, read the instructions to each question booklet, underline any key words or phrases, such as *least, best, outline, describe* and the like. In this way you will tend to answer as requested rather than discover on reviewing your paper that you *listed without describing*, that you selected the *worst* choice rather than the *best* choice, etc.

3) If the examination is of the objective or multiple-choice type – that is, each question will also give a series of possible answers: A, B, C or D, and you are called upon to select the best answer and write the letter next to that answer on your answer paper – it is advisable to start answering each question in turn. There may be anywhere from 50 to 100 such questions in the three or four hours allotted and you can see how much time would be taken if you read through all the questions before beginning to answer any. Furthermore, if you come across a question or group of questions which you know would be difficult to answer, it would undoubtedly affect your handling of all the other questions.

4) If the examination is of the essay type and contains but a few questions, it is a moot point as to whether you should read all the questions before starting to answer any one. Of course, if you are given a choice – say five out of seven and the like – then it is essential to read all the questions so you can eliminate the two that are most difficult. If, however, you are asked to answer all the questions, there may be danger in trying to answer the easiest one first because you may find that you will spend too much time on it. The best technique is to answer the first question, then proceed to the second, etc.

5) Time your answers. Before the exam begins, write down the time it started, then add the time allowed for the examination and write down the time it must be completed, then divide the time available somewhat as follows:
   - If 3-1/2 hours are allowed, that would be 210 minutes. If you have 80 objective-type questions, that would be an average of 2-1/2 minutes per question. Allow yourself no more than 2 minutes per question, or a total of 160 minutes, which will permit about 50 minutes to review.
   - If for the time allotment of 210 minutes there are 7 essay questions to answer, that would average about 30 minutes a question. Give yourself only 25 minutes per question so that you have about 35 minutes to review.

6) The most important instruction is to *read each question* and make sure you know what is wanted. The second most important instruction is to *time yourself properly* so that you answer every question. The third most important instruction is to *answer every question*. Guess if you have to but include something for each question. Remember that you will receive no credit for a blank and will probably receive some credit if you write something in answer to an essay question. If you guess a letter – say "B" for a multiple-choice question – you may have guessed right. If you leave a blank as an answer to a multiple-choice question, the examiners may respect your feelings but it will not add a point to your score. Some exams may penalize you for wrong answers, so in such cases *only*, you may not want to guess unless you have some basis for your answer.

7) Suggestions
   a. Objective-type questions
      1. Examine the question booklet for proper sequence of pages and questions
      2. Read all instructions carefully
      3. Skip any question which seems too difficult; return to it after all other questions have been answered
      4. Apportion your time properly; do not spend too much time on any single question or group of questions

5. Note and underline key words – *all, most, fewest, least, best, worst, same, opposite,* etc.
6. Pay particular attention to negatives
7. Note unusual option, e.g., unduly long, short, complex, different or similar in content to the body of the question
8. Observe the use of "hedging" words – *probably, may, most likely,* etc.
9. Make sure that your answer is put next to the same number as the question
10. Do not second-guess unless you have good reason to believe the second answer is definitely more correct
11. Cross out original answer if you decide another answer is more accurate; do not erase until you are ready to hand your paper in
12. Answer all questions; guess unless instructed otherwise
13. Leave time for review

b. Essay questions
1. Read each question carefully
2. Determine exactly what is wanted. Underline key words or phrases.
3. Decide on outline or paragraph answer
4. Include many different points and elements unless asked to develop any one or two points or elements
5. Show impartiality by giving pros and cons unless directed to select one side only
6. Make and write down any assumptions you find necessary to answer the questions
7. Watch your English, grammar, punctuation and choice of words
8. Time your answers; don't crowd material

8) Answering the essay question

Most essay questions can be answered by framing the specific response around several key words or ideas. Here are a few such key words or ideas:

M's: manpower, materials, methods, money, management
P's: purpose, program, policy, plan, procedure, practice, problems, pitfalls, personnel, public relations

a. Six basic steps in handling problems:
1. Preliminary plan and background development
2. Collect information, data and facts
3. Analyze and interpret information, data and facts
4. Analyze and develop solutions as well as make recommendations
5. Prepare report and sell recommendations
6. Install recommendations and follow up effectiveness

b. Pitfalls to avoid
1. *Taking things for granted* – A statement of the situation does not necessarily imply that each of the elements is necessarily true; for example, a complaint may be invalid and biased so that all that can be taken for granted is that a complaint has been registered

2. *Considering only one side of a situation* – Wherever possible, indicate several alternatives and then point out the reasons you selected the best one
3. *Failing to indicate follow up* – Whenever your answer indicates action on your part, make certain that you will take proper follow-up action to see how successful your recommendations, procedures or actions turn out to be
4. *Taking too long in answering any single question* – Remember to time your answers properly

IX. AFTER THE TEST

Scoring procedures differ in detail among civil service jurisdictions although the general principles are the same. Whether the papers are hand-scored or graded by machine we have described, they are nearly always graded by number. That is, the person who marks the paper knows only the number – never the name – of the applicant. Not until all the papers have been graded will they be matched with names. If other tests, such as training and experience or oral interview ratings have been given, scores will be combined. Different parts of the examination usually have different weights. For example, the written test might count 60 percent of the final grade, and a rating of training and experience 40 percent. In many jurisdictions, veterans will have a certain number of points added to their grades.

After the final grade has been determined, the names are placed in grade order and an eligible list is established. There are various methods for resolving ties between those who get the same final grade – probably the most common is to place first the name of the person whose application was received first. Job offers are made from the eligible list in the order the names appear on it. You will be notified of your grade and your rank as soon as all these computations have been made. This will be done as rapidly as possible.

People who are found to meet the requirements in the announcement are called "eligibles." Their names are put on a list of eligible candidates. An eligible's chances of getting a job depend on how high he stands on this list and how fast agencies are filling jobs from the list.

When a job is to be filled from a list of eligibles, the agency asks for the names of people on the list of eligibles for that job. When the civil service commission receives this request, it sends to the agency the names of the three people highest on this list. Or, if the job to be filled has specialized requirements, the office sends the agency the names of the top three persons who meet these requirements from the general list.

The appointing officer makes a choice from among the three people whose names were sent to him. If the selected person accepts the appointment, the names of the others are put back on the list to be considered for future openings.

That is the rule in hiring from all kinds of eligible lists, whether they are for typist, carpenter, chemist, or something else. For every vacancy, the appointing officer has his choice of any one of the top three eligibles on the list. This explains why the person whose name is on top of the list sometimes does not get an appointment when some of the persons lower on the list do. If the appointing officer chooses the second or third eligible, the No. 1 eligible does not get a job at once, but stays on the list until he is appointed or the list is terminated.

X. HOW TO PASS THE INTERVIEW TEST

The examination for which you applied requires an oral interview test. You have already taken the written test and you are now being called for the interview test – the final part of the formal examination.

You may think that it is not possible to prepare for an interview test and that there are no procedures to follow during an interview. Our purpose is to point out some things you can do in advance that will help you and some good rules to follow and pitfalls to avoid while you are being interviewed.

What is an interview supposed to test?

The written examination is designed to test the technical knowledge and competence of the candidate; the oral is designed to evaluate intangible qualities, not readily measured otherwise, and to establish a list showing the relative fitness of each candidate – as measured against his competitors – for the position sought. Scoring is not on the basis of "right" and "wrong," but on a sliding scale of values ranging from "not passable" to "outstanding." As a matter of fact, it is possible to achieve a relatively low score without a single "incorrect" answer because of evident weakness in the qualities being measured.

Occasionally, an examination may consist entirely of an oral test – either an individual or a group oral. In such cases, information is sought concerning the technical knowledges and abilities of the candidate, since there has been no written examination for this purpose. More commonly, however, an oral test is used to supplement a written examination.

Who conducts interviews?

The composition of oral boards varies among different jurisdictions. In nearly all, a representative of the personnel department serves as chairman. One of the members of the board may be a representative of the department in which the candidate would work. In some cases, "outside experts" are used, and, frequently, a businessman or some other representative of the general public is asked to serve. Labor and management or other special groups may be represented. The aim is to secure the services of experts in the appropriate field.

However the board is composed, it is a good idea (and not at all improper or unethical) to ascertain in advance of the interview who the members are and what groups they represent. When you are introduced to them, you will have some idea of their backgrounds and interests, and at least you will not stutter and stammer over their names.

What should be done before the interview?

While knowledge about the board members is useful and takes some of the surprise element out of the interview, there is other preparation which is more substantive. It *is* possible to prepare for an oral interview – in several ways:

1) Keep a copy of your application and review it carefully before the interview

This may be the only document before the oral board, and the starting point of the interview. Know what education and experience you have listed there, and the sequence and dates of all of it. Sometimes the board will ask you to review the highlights of your experience for them; you should not have to hem and haw doing it.

2) Study the class specification and the examination announcement

Usually, the oral board has one or both of these to guide them. The qualities, characteristics or knowledges required by the position sought are stated in these documents. They offer valuable clues as to the nature of the oral interview. For example, if the job involves supervisory responsibilities, the announcement will usually indicate that knowledge of modern supervisory methods and the qualifications of the candidate as a supervisor will be tested. If so, you can expect such questions, frequently in the form of a hypothetical situation which you are expected to solve. NEVER go into an oral without knowledge of the duties and responsibilities of the job you seek.

3) Think through each qualification required

Try to visualize the kind of questions you would ask if you were a board member. How well could you answer them? Try especially to appraise your own knowledge and background in each area, *measured against the job sought*, and identify any areas in which you are weak. Be critical and realistic – do not flatter yourself.

4) Do some general reading in areas in which you feel you may be weak

For example, if the job involves supervision and your past experience has NOT, some general reading in supervisory methods and practices, particularly in the field of human relations, might be useful. Do NOT study agency procedures or detailed manuals. The oral board will be testing your understanding and capacity, not your memory.

5) Get a good night's sleep and watch your general health and mental attitude

You will want a clear head at the interview. Take care of a cold or any other minor ailment, and of course, no hangovers.

What should be done on the day of the interview?

Now comes the day of the interview itself. Give yourself plenty of time to get there. Plan to arrive somewhat ahead of the scheduled time, particularly if your appointment is in the fore part of the day. If a previous candidate fails to appear, the board might be ready for you a bit early. By early afternoon an oral board is almost invariably behind schedule if there are many candidates, and you may have to wait. Take along a book or magazine to read, or your application to review, but leave any extraneous material in the waiting room when you go in for your interview. In any event, relax and compose yourself.

The matter of dress is important. The board is forming impressions about you – from your experience, your manners, your attitude, and your appearance. Give your personal appearance careful attention. Dress your best, but not your flashiest. Choose conservative, appropriate clothing, and be sure it is immaculate. This is a business interview, and your appearance should indicate that you regard it as such. Besides, being well groomed and properly dressed will help boost your confidence.

Sooner or later, someone will call your name and escort you into the interview room. *This is it.* From here on you are on your own. It is too late for any more preparation. But remember, you asked for this opportunity to prove your fitness, and you are here because your request was granted.

What happens when you go in?

The usual sequence of events will be as follows: The clerk (who is often the board stenographer) will introduce you to the chairman of the oral board, who will introduce you to the other members of the board. Acknowledge the introductions before you sit down. Do not be surprised if you find a microphone facing you or a stenotypist sitting by. Oral interviews are usually recorded in the event of an appeal or other review.

Usually the chairman of the board will open the interview by reviewing the highlights of your education and work experience from your application – primarily for the benefit of the other members of the board, as well as to get the material into the record. Do not interrupt or comment unless there is an error or significant misinterpretation; if that is the case, do not hesitate. But do not quibble about insignificant matters. Also, he will usually ask you some question about your education, experience or your present job – partly to get you to start talking and to establish the interviewing "rapport." He may start the actual questioning, or turn it over to one of the other members. Frequently, each member undertakes the questioning on a particular area, one in which he is perhaps most competent, so you can expect each member to participate in the examination. Because time is limited, you may also expect some rather abrupt switches in the direction the questioning takes, so do not be upset by it. Normally, a board member will not pursue a single line of questioning unless he discovers a particular strength or weakness.

After each member has participated, the chairman will usually ask whether any member has any further questions, then will ask you if you have anything you wish to add. Unless you are expecting this question, it may floor you. Worse, it may start you off on an extended, extemporaneous speech. The board is not usually seeking more information. The question is principally to offer you a last opportunity to present further qualifications or to indicate that you have nothing to add. So, if you feel that a significant qualification or characteristic has been overlooked, it is proper to point it out in a sentence or so. Do not compliment the board on the thoroughness of their examination – they have been sketchy, and you know it. If you wish, merely say, "No thank you, I have nothing further to add." This is a point where you can "talk yourself out" of a good impression or fail to present an important bit of information. Remember, *you close the interview yourself.*

The chairman will then say, "That is all, Mr. _____, thank you." Do not be startled; the interview is over, and quicker than you think. Thank him, gather your belongings and take your leave. Save your sigh of relief for the other side of the door.

How to put your best foot forward

Throughout this entire process, you may feel that the board individually and collectively is trying to pierce your defenses, seek out your hidden weaknesses and embarrass and confuse you. Actually, this is not true. They are obliged to make an appraisal of your qualifications for the job you are seeking, and they want to see you in your best light. Remember, they must interview all candidates and a non-cooperative candidate may become a failure in spite of their best efforts to bring out his qualifications. Here are 15 suggestions that will help you:

1) Be natural – Keep your attitude confident, not cocky

If you are not confident that you can do the job, do not expect the board to be. Do not apologize for your weaknesses, try to bring out your strong points. The board is interested in a positive, not negative, presentation. Cockiness will antagonize any board member and make him wonder if you are covering up a weakness by a false show of strength.

2) Get comfortable, but don't lounge or sprawl

Sit erectly but not stiffly. A careless posture may lead the board to conclude that you are careless in other things, or at least that you are not impressed by the importance of the occasion. Either conclusion is natural, even if incorrect. Do not fuss with your clothing, a pencil or an ashtray. Your hands may occasionally be useful to emphasize a point; do not let them become a point of distraction.

3) Do not wisecrack or make small talk

This is a serious situation, and your attitude should show that you consider it as such. Further, the time of the board is limited – they do not want to waste it, and neither should you.

4) Do not exaggerate your experience or abilities

In the first place, from information in the application or other interviews and sources, the board may know more about you than you think. Secondly, you probably will not get away with it. An experienced board is rather adept at spotting such a situation, so do not take the chance.

5) If you know a board member, do not make a point of it, yet do not hide it

Certainly you are not fooling him, and probably not the other members of the board. Do not try to take advantage of your acquaintanceship – it will probably do you little good.

6) Do not dominate the interview

Let the board do that. They will give you the clues – do not assume that you have to do all the talking. Realize that the board has a number of questions to ask you, and do not try to take up all the interview time by showing off your extensive knowledge of the answer to the first one.

7) Be attentive

You only have 20 minutes or so, and you should keep your attention at its sharpest throughout. When a member is addressing a problem or question to you, give him your undivided attention. Address your reply principally to him, but do not exclude the other board members.

8) Do not interrupt

A board member may be stating a problem for you to analyze. He will ask you a question when the time comes. Let him state the problem, and wait for the question.

9) Make sure you understand the question

Do not try to answer until you are sure what the question is. If it is not clear, restate it in your own words or ask the board member to clarify it for you. However, do not haggle about minor elements.

10) Reply promptly but not hastily

A common entry on oral board rating sheets is "candidate responded readily," or "candidate hesitated in replies." Respond as promptly and quickly as you can, but do not jump to a hasty, ill-considered answer.

11) Do not be peremptory in your answers

A brief answer is proper – but do not fire your answer back. That is a losing game from your point of view. The board member can probably ask questions much faster than you can answer them.

12) Do not try to create the answer you think the board member wants

He is interested in what kind of mind you have and how it works – not in playing games. Furthermore, he can usually spot this practice and will actually grade you down on it.

13) Do not switch sides in your reply merely to agree with a board member

Frequently, a member will take a contrary position merely to draw you out and to see if you are willing and able to defend your point of view. Do not start a debate, yet do not surrender a good position. If a position is worth taking, it is worth defending.

14) Do not be afraid to admit an error in judgment if you are shown to be wrong
The board knows that you are forced to reply without any opportunity for careful consideration. Your answer may be demonstrably wrong. If so, admit it and get on with the interview.

15) Do not dwell at length on your present job
The opening question may relate to your present assignment. Answer the question but do not go into an extended discussion. You are being examined for a *new* job, not your present one. As a matter of fact, try to phrase ALL your answers in terms of the job for which you are being examined.

Basis of Rating
Probably you will forget most of these "do's" and "don'ts" when you walk into the oral interview room. Even remembering them all will not ensure you a passing grade. Perhaps you did not have the qualifications in the first place. But remembering them will help you to put your best foot forward, without treading on the toes of the board members.

Rumor and popular opinion to the contrary notwithstanding, an oral board wants you to make the best appearance possible. They know you are under pressure – but they also want to see how you respond to it as a guide to what your reaction would be under the pressures of the job you seek. They will be influenced by the degree of poise you display, the personal traits you show and the manner in which you respond.

ABOUT THIS BOOK

This book contains tests divided into Examination Sections. Go through each test, answering every question in the margin. We have also attached a sample answer sheet at the back of the book that can be removed and used. At the end of each test look at the answer key and check your answers. On the ones you got wrong, look at the right answer choice and learn. Do not fill in the answers first. Do not memorize the questions and answers, but understand the answer and principles involved. On your test, the questions will likely be different from the samples. Questions are changed and new ones added. If you understand these past questions you should have success with any changes that arise. Tests may consist of several types of questions. We have additional books on each subject should more study be advisable or necessary for you. Finally, the more you study, the better prepared you will be. This book is intended to be the last thing you study before you walk into the examination room. Prior study of relevant texts is also recommended. NLC publishes some of these in our Fundamental Series. Knowledge and good sense are important factors in passing your exam. Good luck also helps. So now study this Passbook, absorb the material contained within and take that knowledge into the examination. Then do your best to pass that exam.

EXAMINATION SECTION

EXAMINATION SECTION
TEST 1

DIRECTIONS: Each question or incomplete statement is followed by several suggested answers or completions. Select the one that BEST answers the question or completes the statement. *PRINT THE LETTER OF THE CORRECT ANSWER IN THE SPACE AT THE RIGHT.*

1. When instructing newly appointed stock assistants in the duties pertaining to the storage and handling of supplies, a stockman should NOT

    A. take their knowledge of procedures for granted
    B. refer to material by the class number
    C. mention the possibility of accidents in the storeroom
    D. permit questions after he has given his instructions

1._____

2. Assume that a stockman constantly reports his stock assistants for violating rules and for doing poor work. This practice by the stockman is

    A. *good,* because it shows that he is able to maintain effective discipline
    B. *good,* because it shows that he knows what is going on in his area
    C. *poor,* becauset it is his responsibility to help them correct their errors
    D. *poor,* because he is expected to overlook many of these violations

2._____

3. Assume that a stock assistant under your supervision fell off a ladder and apparently suffered a leg fracture. While waiting for a doctor to arrive, you should

    A. rub the leg to maintain proper circulation
    B. apply splints if you think they are necessary
    C. have him try to walk so you can see how badly he is hurt
    D. make him as comfortable as possible without moving him unnecessarily

3._____

4. A good way for a stockman to break in a new stock assistant is to

    A. leave him alone until he gets the feel of the work
    B. personally show him all phases of the job
    C. assign a capable stock assistant to work with him and instruct him
    D. assign him to spend his time watching how the other men perform their work

4._____

5. When a stock assistant is filling more than one requisition at a time, he should be alert to the greater possibility of

    A. a space shortage
    B. running out of work
    C. error
    D. fatigue

5._____

6. Assume that you are a stockman, and a stock assistant under your supervision strongly objects to your instructions on how to load a truck.
If, after listening to this man, you still feel that you are right, you should

    A. get the opinion of another stockman
    B. take this assistant off the job immediately
    C. reprimand the man for questioning your competence
    D. tell the man to load the truck in accordance with your instructions

6._____

1

7. If the men under your supervision have to do a lot of heavy work in warm weather, it is MOST advisable to

   A. stagger their lunch hours
   B. have the men report to work early
   C. give them more frequent rest periods than usual
   D. eliminate some of the record keeping requirements

8. Assume that you are a stockman and you find that a new stock assistant made an error in filling a requisition, but later found the mistake and corrected it.
   The MOST advisable course of action for you to take is to

   A. warn him to be more careful
   B. ignore the entire situation unless it happens again
   C. show him how he can avoid such a mistake in the future
   D. review all the work of the man who made the error

9. Placing extra weight on the rear of a fork-lift truck which is carrying an overload is

   A. *good,* because this will prevent the truck from tipping
   B. *poor,* because this will prevent the mast from tilting
   C. *good,* because the truck may then be safely operated at a higher speed
   D. *poor,* because it strains the tires, axles, and motor

10. The CHIEF reason for not letting oily rags accumulate in storage bins is that they

    A. look dirty
    B. may drip oil onto the floor
    C. may start a fire by spontaneous combustion
    D. take up valuable storage space

11. A newly appointed stockman trying to complete a job finds that he is being delayed by a stock assistant who keeps talking about his after-hours social life.
    It would be BEST for the new stockman to

    A. ignore the stock assistant and continue with his job
    B. ask the foreman to transfer the stock assistant to another location
    C. tell the stock assistant that he has no time to talk since he must complete his job without delay
    D. go along with the conversation and explain to the foreman the reason for the delay in the completion of the job

12. Of the following, the BEST way to put out a gasoline fire is to use

    A. a carbon dioxide extinguisher
    B. compressed air
    C. water
    D. rags to smother the blaze

13. You find that your foreman has a tendency to give you verbal orders which lack sufficient detail and clarity. As a stockman, the BEST procedure to follow is to

    A. complain to his superior about this condition
    B. insist that he give all of his orders in writing

C. ask for clarification at the time you receive orders from him
D. go back to him repeatedly for information until he realizes his error

14. Of the following, the factor which is MOST likely to make a stockman *accident prone* is

    A. working with a new stock assistant
    B. being reassigned to an unfamiliar satellite storeroom
    C. coming to work tired and fatigued regularly
    D. having many years of service in the storeroom

15. If you observe an accident involving injury to a fellow worker, the FIRST thing you should do is to

    A. take the victim to a nearby hospital
    B. prepare a detailed accident report
    C. get the names of at least two witnesses
    D. render all possible first-aid to the victim

16. An example of *good housekeeping* in a storeroom would be to

    A. make certain that some pieces of every item remain in stock
    B. issue old stock from the bottom of the bin first
    C. keep storeroom aisles clear of obstructions
    D. keep air brake components in a special room

17. Of the following, the factor which is generally MOST important when deciding where to store an item is the

    A. capacity of the storeroom
    B. notations on the MRR
    C. value of the item
    D. frequency of requests for this item

18. Of the following items, the GREATEST precaution against theft should be taken for

    A. a date stamper machine
    B. 12 foot lengths of 1 1/2 inch brass pipe
    C. sacks of cement
    D. small tools

19. If a maintainer asks a stockman for a can of carbon tetra-chloride to be used for cleaning electrical switches, the stockman should advise the maintainer that

    A. regulations forbid the use of this material for cleaning
    B. the stockman will have to look up the number before he can pull the item from stock
    C. the maintainer will need his foreman's written approval for this particular item
    D. this item can be obtained commercially by the maintainer's foreman

20. If the re-order point is obtained by multiplying the monthly rate of consumption by the lead time (in months) and adding the minimum balance, then for an item which has a minimum balance of 100, a monthly rate of consumption of 150 and a lead time of 3 months, the re-order is

    A. 100   B. 150   C. 450   D. 550

21. A requisition calls for 2 1/4 gross of U-bolts. The number of U-bolts to be issued is

    A. 288   B. 324   C. 432   D. 648

22. A stock assistant has to pick up a tray of brake shoes. The combined weight of tray and brake shoes is 4,000 pounds. Assume that each brake shoe weighs 40 pounds and the tray weighs 240 pounds.
    The number of brake shoes in the tray is MOST NEARLY

    A. 88   B. 94   C. 100   D. 106

23. A maintainer requisitions two pieces of lumber, one 1" x 6" x 12' long, and the other 1" x 3" x 16' long. The TOTAL number of board feet is

    A. 10   B. 12   C. 16   D. 28

24. Assume that you have received 7 cartons, each containing 12 boxes of an item. If each carton costs $21.00, the cost per box is

    A. $0.35   B. $1.75   C. $1.90   D. $3.00

25. Two men are able to fully load a truck with 20 crates in one hour.
    To FULLY load 20 such trucks with four such men, it would take _____ hour(s).

    A. 1   B. 5   C. 10   D. 20

26. A box 6" x 8" x 9" has a volume of _____ cubic feet.

    A. 1/4   B. 1/2   C. 2/3   D. 3/4

27. A stockman checks on a shipment of 1000 articles by inspecting a sampling of 50 articles. Of the sample, 2 articles are wholly defective and 3 more are partly defective.
    On the basis of this sample, the percentage of completely acceptable articles in the entire shipment is

    A. 10%   B. 90%   C. 94%   D. 96%

28. In order to fill 160 eight-ounce bottles, the number of quarts needed is

    A. 4   B. 20   C. 32   D. 40

29. A floor space 6'6" wide and 7'3" long has an area measuring MOST NEARLY _____ square feet.

    A. 43   B. 45   C. 47   D. 50

30. If a steel bar stock weighs 2 pounds/foot and only two 12'4" and three 8'5" pieces are in stock, the total weight of this stock is MOST NEARLY _____ pounds.

    A. 45   B. 50   C. 100   D. 150

31. The bill for a certain type of desk is listed as $400.00, less successive discounts of 25%, 15%, and 5%.
    The amount to be paid for the desk is APPROXIMATELY

    A. $355.00   B. $240.00   C. $220.00   D. $160.00

32. A reel of cable weighs 1000 lbs.
If the empty reel weighs 287 lbs. and the cable weighs 7.19 lbs. per ft., the number of feet of cable on the reel is MOST NEARLY

    A. 100   B. 120   C. 140   D. 180

33. If it takes 2 stock assistants 3 days to do a certain job, then the time it should take 3 stock assistants working at the same speed to do the same job is MOST NEARLY _____ day(s).

    A. 1   B. 1 1/2   C. 2   D. 2 1/2

34. The number of sheets in a ream of paper is MOST NEARLY

    A. 500   B. 1000   C. 1200   D. 1500

35. If an employee tells the authority to deduct 3% of his $234.40 weekly salary for a savings bond, the MINIMUM number of weekly deductions required to get enough money to buy a bond costing $18.75 is

    A. 2   B. 3   C. 4   D. 5

36. Assume that you, as a stockman, have to move twelve 60-pound cartons a distance of about 200 feet, and each carton measures 12" x 24" x 36".
Of the following, the method of moving the cartons that is ordinarily the BEST is to

    A. load them on a skid and push the skid
    B. load them on a pallet and use a fork-lift truck
    C. load them on a trailer and pull it with a tractor
    D. assign two stock assistants to carry the cartons

37. A logical reason for stocking long rectangular tubes in layers, with the first layer lengthwise and the next layer crosswise, is to

    A. prevent toppling
    B. conserve space
    C. make inspection easier
    D. make it easier to count the tubes

38. For the GREATEST economy in transporting stock within a storeroom, it is BEST to

    A. transport as large a load as can be safely moved at one time
    B. use men instead of machines wherever possible
    C. divide the load into as many easily managed units as possible
    D. use conveyor belts for most transporting

39. The first consideration in loading a truck which is making deliveries to several different locations should be to arrange the stock according to

    A. the value of the commodity
    B. weight
    C. size
    D. destination

40. Assume that you are in charge of a group of four stock assistants who are to carry a 6" diameter iron pipe, 21 feet long, from one location to another.
Of the following, the BEST method of carrying the pipe is to have

    A. the men arrange themselves in order of height along the pipe so that it may be carried on the shoulders of all the men
    B. two men stand at each end of the pipe in order to lift it onto the shoulders of the two strongest men
    C. the men arrange themselves at equal distances along one side of the pipe and carry it at their sides
    D. the men arrange themselves at equal distances on opposite sides of the pipe and carry it at waist height

40.____

KEY (CORRECT ANSWERS)

1. A	11. C	21. B	31. B
2. C	12. A	22. B	32. A
3. D	13. C	23. A	33. C
4. C	14. C	24. B	34. A
5. C	15. D	25. C	35. B
6. D	16. C	26. A	36. B
7. C	17. D	27. B	37. A
8. C	18. D	28. D	38. A
9. D	19. A	29. C	39. D
10. C	20. D	30. C	40. C

TEST 2

DIRECTIONS: Each question or incomplete statement is followed by several suggested answers or completions. Select the one that BEST answers the question or completes the statement. *PRINT THE LETTER OF THE CORRECT ANSWER IN THE SPACE AT THE RIGHT.*

1. If a stockman notices a loose lighting fixture he thinks may fall from the ceiling, he should   1.____

   A. get a stepladder and tie the fixture up temporarily with a cord
   B. find the switch and turn the light off
   C. tell his foreman about the fixture
   D. forget it because the light maintainer should find it

2. A stock assistant accidentally spatters acid into his eye. First aid treatment for the eye should consist of the immediate application of   2.____

   A. cold water   B. a bandage
   C. baking soda   D. vaseline

3. The BEST way to lift a heavy object is to   3.____

   A. keep legs far apart and straight, bending at the waist to grasp the object
   B. place the feet shoulder width apart and bend at the knees to reach down to the object
   C. keep legs straight and close together, bending at the waist to grasp the object
   D. get a good footing, and with legs straight, bend at waist to reach down and quickly lift the object

4. When summoning an ambulance for an injured person, of the following information, it is MOST important to give the   4.____

   A. name of the injured person
   B. cause of the accident
   C. nature of the injuries
   D. location of the injured person

5. Fire extinguishers are provided in storerooms to be used in case of fire.
   To make sure that these extinguishers are ALWAYS in readiness, they should be periodically   5.____

   A. used   B. inspected   C. replaced   D. rotated

6. The MAIN reason for requiring an injured employee to submit an accident report is so that   6.____

   A. the employee may be properly reprimanded
   B. the employee may be given the proper medical attention
   C. safeguards may be provided against future such accidents
   D. it will remind the employee to be more careful in the future

7. In the interest of safety, it is good practice for storeroom employees to   7.____

   A. wear safety helmets when loading shelves
   B. work only in teams of two or more

7

C. consider the various possibilities of accidents on each job
D. wait for the foreman before starting on any job

8. An item which could become a hazard if stored in the hot sun is a

   A. drum of freon refrigerant
   B. drum of Prestone anti-freeze
   C. bag of cement
   D. bag of rock salt

9. Water should NOT be used to put out _____ fires.

   A. wood
   B. paper
   C. fabric
   D. electrical

10. When an accident victim is unconscious, it is BEST to

    A. keep him warm
    B. give him hot coffee
    C. apply ice to his neck
    D. raise him to a sitting position

11. When issuing flammable material such as gasoline, the MOST important safety precaution to be observed is to

    A. dispense this material only in well-ventilated areas
    B. dispense this material only in approved containers
    C. blow out the empty containers with compressed air
    D. dispense this material only if a soda acid fire extinguisher is at hand

12. Assume that the inventory card shows a much smaller quantity of a certain item than you count in the bin. The MOST advisable action for you to take FIRST is to

    A. consult your supervisor
    B. recheck the figures on the inventory card
    C. correct the final figure on the inventory card
    D. review all requisitions issued since the last physical inventory count

13. Assume that you, as stockman, count 43 motor control resistors while taking inventory and your stock assistant counts 47.
    In this case, you should

    A. recount the items together
    B. regard your own count as correct since you are the senior man
    C. take the average of the two figures since the difference is slight
    D. accept the stock assistant's figure since it doesn't make any difference

14. A stockman discovers that some of the material in one of the bins has been misplaced by a newly appointed stock assistant.
    The stockman should

    A. ignore the incident
    B. bring the matter to the attention of the foreman
    C. impress on the stock assistant that he should be more careful
    D. give the stock assistant a different assignment

15. To avoid damage when opening wooden crates containing small, fragile items, it is generally BEST first to open the   15._____

    A. top   B. front   C. back   D. bottom

16. Scrap metal is frequently referred to as ferrous and non-ferrous.   16._____
    This distinction is based on the metal's

    A. quality   B. monetary value
    C. chemical composition   D. physical condition

17. Sheets of coated abrasive cloth come in standard unit packages of either 250 sheets   17._____
    each or 500 sheets each, depending on the

    A. grit number of the cloth
    B. size of the sheet
    C. manufacturer of the cloth
    D. size of the order

18. A good stockman should know when to refer a matter to his foreman.   18._____
    Of the following, a situation which a stockman should refer to his foreman occurs whenever

    A. the stockman believes the cost of an item is excessive
    B. a certain stock is running low
    C. a foreman from another department personally submits a requisition
    D. the stockman believes that a requisition contains more material than needed

19. A maintainer approaches a busy stockman with whom he is friendly and says that he   19._____
    needs a critical piece of equipment immediately. The stockman explains where the piece is stored and suggests to the maintainer that he can help out by picking it out of stock himself while the stockman completes the order he is working on.
    This suggestion by the stockman is

    A. *good,* because it shows that he is a cooperative employee
    B. *poor,* because he is permitting someone else to perform his duty
    C. *good,* because it shows that he is an efficient stockman
    D. *poor,* because the maintainer may not be able to identify the correct piece

20. A stock assistant asks you what is meant by a 12-24 hacksaw blade.   20._____
    You should tell him that the number 12 refers to the

    A. blade length   B. blade thickness
    C. maximum stroke   D. no. of teeth/inch

21. The MAIN reason for the requirement that all accidents must be reported, no matter how   21._____
    slight the injury may appear, is that

    A. the safety committee needs accurate statistical data
    B. employees should be trained to report accidents properly
    C. an employee may not realize that his injury could be serious
    D. disciplinary action can be taken against the employee responsible for the accident

22. When a stockman is moving a bulky load with a power lift truck, he should NOT

    A. drive in reverse if his load blocks forward visibility
    B. turn off the engine when the lift truck is to be parked
    C. drive in the forward direction when his load blocks forward visibility
    D. block the wheels when the lift truck is to be parked

23. The gill is a unit of measure for

    A. length   B. area   C. weight   D. volume

24. If you know today that you will have to be absent tomorrow, you should

    A. tell your foreman about it today
    B. say nothing about it unless somebody asks
    C. stay late today to get ahead on your work
    D. tell your foreman why you were absent after you return to work

25. In some cases, when a reorder of certain material is received, it is necessary that the new material be stored in such a way that the old stock will be issued first. This method is MOST essential with material which

    A. moves slowly
    B. deteriorates with age
    C. may become obsolete
    D. is ordered in large quantities

26. If a certain type of screw comes in a wooden box which has written on it the words *Net Weight 20 pounds,* it means that the

    A. weight of 20 pounds is approximate
    B. screws and box together weigh 20 pounds
    C. screws alone weigh 20 pounds
    D. box alone weighs 20 pounds

27. It is normally good practice to store small items in their original containers whenever possible because this practice

    A. decreases handling
    B. makes it easier to inspect the item
    C. eliminates the need for shelves and bins
    D. eliminates the necessity of checking incoming shipments of the item

28. In checking a large incoming shipment of special machine screws, the BEST practice to follow is to

    A. count the total number of cartons received and check the contents of some of the cartons
    B. open all cartons and count the exact number of units in each carton
    C. count only the total number of cartons received and assume that the number of units inside each carton is correct
    D. count the total number of units only in those cartons where there is some doubt

29. One of the MAIN reasons for keeping a perpetual inventory is that it

    A. enables stock to be issued more quickly
    B. eliminates the need for a physical inventory
    C. helps reduce the number of errors made in filling requisitions
    D. provides an up-to-date record of stock on hand at all times

30. One-inch diameter, square neck, round head carriage bolts are purchased

    A. by the dozen
    B. by the gross
    C. in units of pounds
    D. in units of 100

31. The form used to direct a vendor to furnish material in accordance with his bid is the

    A. delivery memorandum
    B. acceptance and order
    C. shipping instructions
    D. replenishment requisition

32. The form used for reporting receipt of repaired materials sent out for overhaul by contractors, or material ordered for special work or jobs, is the

    A. material receiving report
    B. delivery memorandum
    C. material transfer record
    D. direct charge report

33. The form used for withdrawal of material from a storeroom is the

    A. delivery memorandum
    B. requisition on stores
    C. material transfer record
    D. material permit

34. The form used to transfer material between storerooms is the

    A. delivery memorandum
    B. material receiving report
    C. material transfer record
    D. direct charge report

35. The form used for replenishing material at satellite storerooms from the main storeroom is the

    A. delivery memorandum
    B. informal requisition on stores
    C. requisition on stores
    D. replenishment requisition

36. Of the following, the form which is issued to truck drivers who have picked up material at storerooms is the

    A. material receiving report
    B. freight and express charge receipt
    C. material permit
    D. direct charge report

37. The form used to request the purchase of items of material not previously ordered or carried in storeroom stock is the

    A. informal requisition on stores
    B. requisition on stores
    C. shipping memorandum
    D. replenishment requisition

38. The form used for sending material out for repair, for returning of rejected material, or for exchanging of material is the

    A. shipping memorandum
    B. requisition on purchasing agent
    C. delivery memorandum
    D. freight and express charge receipt

39. On an adjustment of inventory form, the MOST important information is that which gives the

    A. unit price of the item
    B. number and location of the storeroom
    C. actual count of the material on hand
    D. name of the person who checked the item

40. A certain item on a requisition is identified by the number, 27-22-0300. The 27 in this number refers to the

    A. class of the item
    B. exact size and weight of the item
    C. number of items to be supplied on the requisition
    D. year in which the item was requisitioned

KEY (CORRECT ANSWERS)

1.	C	11.	B	21.	C	31.	B
2.	A	12.	C	22.	C	32.	B
3.	B	13.	A	23.	D	33.	B
4.	D	14.	C	24.	A	34.	C
5.	B	15.	A	25.	B	35.	D
6.	C	16.	C	26.	C	36.	C
7.	C	17.	A	27.	A	37.	A
8.	A	18.	B	28.	A	38.	A
9.	D	19.	B	29.	D	39.	C
10.	A	20.	A	30.	D	40.	A

EXAMINATION SECTION
TEST 1

DIRECTIONS: Each question or incomplete statement is followed by several suggested answers or completions. Select the one that BEST answers the question or completes the statement. *PRINT THE LETTER OF THE CORRECT ANSWER IN THE SPACE AT THE RIGHT.*

1. The MAIN reason for keeping storeroom aisles clear of obstruction is to prevent

    A. injury to employees
    B. damage to stock
    C. loss of material
    D. complaints from the foreman

2. When storing material, the stockman should pay GREATEST attention to

    A. the condition of the bin
    B. who delivered the shipment
    C. the number of items
    D. the classification number

3. The number of pounds in a long ton is

    A. 2000   B. 2240   C. 2400   D. 4000

4. A stockman should store material as compactly as possible MAINLY

    A. for easy removal
    B. to avoid damage
    C. to save space
    D. to prevent deterioration

5. To avoid discrepancies as to the number of items shipped, a stockman unpacking small fragile items packed in excelsior should be careful

    A. not to drop any of the items
    B. to check the condition of each item
    C. to place the items in their proper storeroom location
    D. that none of the items remain in the excelsior

6. When issuing inflammable material such as gasoline, the MOST important safety precaution to be observed is to

    A. be certain that some remains in stock
    B. avoid waste
    C. be certain that the requisition is properly filled
    D. dispense only in approved containers

7. If you find that your foreman has a tendency to give you verbal orders which lack sufficient detail and clarity, it would be BEST for you to

    A. insist that he give all his orders to you in writing
    B. obtain clarification from him at the time you receive his orders by asking for essential details
    C. complain to the assistant supervisor about this situation
    D. use your best judgment as that is all that can be expected

13

8. If there is a man in your storeroom who has frequent accidents, a logical assumption would be that this man is

    A. simply unlucky
    B. physically unfit for his job
    C. mentally unfit for his job
    D. violating too many safety rules

9. When an unusual situation arises and it would take too long to contact a superior to check the method of handling the situation, the BEST procedure is to

    A. check through the records for a possible similar case
    B. let another stockman handle the matter
    C. take no action
    D. act according to your own best judgment

10. In some cases, when a reorder of certain material is received, it is necessary that the new material be stored in such a way that the old stock will be issued first. This method is MOST essential with material which

    A. may become obsolete
    B. deteriorates with age
    C. is ordered in large quantities
    D. moves slowly

11. A newly assigned stockman is MOST likely to secure the respect of his assistants if he

    A. overlooks minor infractions of rules
    B. permits them to take it easy
    C. fraternizes with them after hours'
    D. shows a thorough knowledge of the job

12. A stockman receiving a shipment of material notices that it differs from the description on the order. He should

    A. accept the shipment without comment
    B. reject the shipment
    C. note the difference in the body of the MRR
    D. use another form in place of the MRR

Questions 13-20.

DIRECTIONS: Questions 13 through 20, inclusive, in Column I are articles stocked in the storeroom, each of which is usually dispensed by one of the quantity-units listed in Column II. For each article in Column I, select the proper quantity-unit from Column II.

	COLUMN I		COLUMN II	
13.	Acid core solder	A.	Pieces	13._____
14.	Creosote	B.	Pounds	14._____
15.	Black iron pipe	C.	Feet	15._____
16.	Ball peen hammers	D.	Gallons	16._____
17.	Whiting			17._____
18.	Lag screws			18._____
19.	Linseed oil			19._____
20.	2 1/2 fire hose			20._____

21. When storing rock salt, precautions should be taken against   21._____

   A. dryness
   B. proximity to inflammable material
   C. open flame
   D. dampness

22. An important advantage of rotating the individual work assignments among a group of   22._____
    men who all hold the same title is that

   A. it removes the opportunity for the men to become lax
   B. no one can be accused of partiality
   C. all the men will become familiar with the different jobs
   D. the foreman will be relieved of responsibility

23. When making written reports, it is MOST important that they be   23._____

   A. brief   B. accurate as to facts
   C. well-worded   D. submitted immediately

24. A requisition calls for 4 1/2 gross of electric connectors. The number of connectors to be   24._____
    issued is

   A. 54   B. 324   C. 648   D. 864

25. A crate measures 3 x 4 x 5 feet. The number of cubic feet in this crate is MOST NEARLY   25._____
    _____ cu.ft.

   A. 12   B. 15   C. 20   D. 60

26. A stockman is NOT expected to assume much supervisory responsibility because   26._____

   A. he usually does unimportant work
   B. his rate of pay is small
   C. he is not capable
   D. other employees are assigned for this purpose

27. The basic reason why unauthorized employees are prevented from entering the storerooms is to minimize

   A. theft
   B. accidents
   C. favoritism
   D. crowding

28. A stockman should contact his foreman whenever

   A. an issuing foreman personally submits a requisition
   B. he believes the cost of an item is excessive
   C. a certain stock is running low
   D. he fills a requisition

29. A stock assistant receiving a requisition for an item which is not in stock should

   A. substitute a comparable item
   B. file the requisition until such time as the item is on hand
   C. investigate to determine if the item is on order
   D. destroy requisition so it cannot be misused

30. The LEAST desirable thing to use to put out a very small rubbish fire in a small unventilated room is

   A. carbon tetrachloride
   B. water
   C. sand
   D. carbon dioxide

31. A stockman whose regular rate is $9.27 per hour worked overtime for 2 1/2 hours. The additional gross pay he should receive for this work is

   A. $13.92   B. $23.19   C. $34.77   D. $46.35

32. The last entry on a card containing a perpetual inventory of material should show the total amount of this material

   A. on order
   B. in stock
   C. received
   D. disbursed

33. An accurate stock record of material in a storeroom is essential to prevent

   A. misinformation
   B. errors in issuing material
   C. pilferage
   D. waste of material by the using department

34. If it takes 2 stockmen 3 days to do a certain sorting job, then the time it should take 3 stockmen working at the same speed to do the same job is MOST NEARLY _____ day(s).

   A. 1/2   B. 1   C. 2   D. 2 1/2

35. Fire extinguishers are provided in storerooms to be used in case of fire. To make sure that these extinguishers are always ready, they should be periodically

   A. inspected   B. used   C. rotated   D. replaced

36. Items are sometimes broken in shipping. This breakage is MOST likely caused by   36._____

    A. rough handling in transit
    B. the fragile nature of the item
    C. incorrect packing
    D. the poor quality of the item

37. A shop maintenance gang requisitioned a new 48" pipe wrench while working on a water   37._____
    line. A few days later, the wrench was returned to the storeroom.
    The MRS should indicate the wrench as

    A. unused   B. used   C. scrap   D. salvage

38. The number of sheets in a ream of paper is   38._____

    A. 500   B. 1000   C. 3500   D. 5000

39. Of the sizes given, the COARSEST grade of sandpaper is   39._____

    A. 0   B. 00   C. 1   D. 2

40. An accident victim with an injured spine should be   40._____

    A. moved only if absolutely necessary
    B. immediately carried to a doctor
    C. turned over on his stomach
    D. given artificial respiration

KEY (CORRECT ANSWERS)

1. A	11. D	21. D	31. C
2. D	12. C	22. C	32. B
3. B	13. B	23. B	33. A
4. C	14. D	24. C	34. C
5. D	15. C	25. D	35. A
6. D	16. A	26. D	36. C
7. B	17. B	27. A	37. B
8. D	18. A	28. C	38. A
9. D	19. D	29. C	39. D
10. B	20. A,C	30. A	40. A

TEST 2

DIRECTIONS: Each question or incomplete statement is followed by several suggested answers or completions. Select the one that BEST answers the question or completes the statement. *PRINT THE LETTER OF THE CORRECT ANSWER IN THE SPACE AT THE RIGHT.*

Questions 1-8.

DIRECTIONS: Questions 1 through 8, inclusive, in Column I are articles stocked in the storeroom, each of which is normally carried under one of the classifications listed in Column II. For each article in Column I, select the proper classification from Column II.

COLUMN I	COLUMN II
1. Plastic wood	A. Hardware
2. Date stamper machine	B. Broom
3. Scrub brush	C. Paint
4. Red lead	D. Stationery
5. Disinfectant	
6. Window chain	
7. Rope	
8. Carbon paper	

9. The MOST important reason for giving complete details on an accident report is because this will
    A. aid in the defense of compensation claims
    B. aid in the stocking of first-aid kits with materials for all types of accidents
    C. be of assistance in preventing future accidents
    D. keep supervision informed on storeroom conditions

9.____

10. Shelves are employed in storerooms for storing materials in order to
    A. permit careful piling of material
    B. fully utilize vertical space
    C. avoid dampness
    D. reserve out-of-the-way space for bulky material

10.____

11. An efficient stockman is one who
    A. has the full cooperation of the stock assistant
    B. is always doing something
    C. performs his work in a conscientious manner
    D. is always in favor with the foreman

11.____

12. Of the following metals, the LIGHTEST in pounds per cubic foot is		12.____

   A. iron	B. brass	C. zinc	D. magnesium

Questions 13-19.

   DIRECTIONS: Questions 13 through 19, inclusive, in Column I are articles stocked in the storeroom, each of which would be cut with one of the hand tools listed in Column II. For each question in Column I, select the proper tool from Column II.

   COLUMN I					COLUMN II

13. 1 1/2" brass pipe			A. Hacksaw		13.____

14. #14 polyethylene covered wire	B. Shears		14.____

15. 16 mesh wire screen cloth		C. Knife		15.____

16. 1/2" aluminum tubing		D. Cutting pliers	16.____

17. #20 gage zinc sheet							17.____

18. 3/4" nylon rope							18.____

19. Hairfelt								19.____

20. A stockman, seeing one of the assistant stockmen coming down a ladder carrying a large carton of lamp bulbs in both hands, should caution the assistant against this procedure MAINLY because the		20.____

   A. lamps may fall and break
   B. assistant is not holding on
   C. large carton is too heavy
   D. assistant did not look before coming down

21. A maintainer, waiting for service at the stockroom window, complains to the stock assistant about the service.		21.____
   A nearby stockman, hearing the complaint, should

   A. refrain from becoming involved
   B. try to determine the reason for the complaint
   C. call it to the attention of the foreman
   D. request the maintainer to return later on in the day

22. In assigning a suitable place in the stockroom for storing a particular item, the LEAST important factor to consider is		22.____

   A. the importance of the sections using it
   B. its fragility
   C. the frequency of requests for it
   D. its size

23. Ten copper negative rail track bonds, which had been sawed off in a rail renewal job, were turned in at a storeroom. The MRS should indicate the bonds as   23._____

   A. salvage   B. used   C. scrap   D. unused

24. A stock assistant who is continually non-cooperative should   24._____

   A. be assigned to undesirable jobs only
   B. be recommended for a caution
   C. never be allowed to work overtime
   D. always be assigned to work alone

25. A stock assistant asks you what is meant by a number 10 wood screw. You should tell him that the number 10 indicates only the   25._____

   A. threads per inch   B. type of head
   C. diameter of the screw   D. length of the screw

Questions 26-32.

   DIRECTIONS: Questions 26 through 32, inclusive, in Column I are incomplete requisitions on stores, each of which lacks the stock number PLUS one of the missing elements listed in Column II. Indicate the letter preceding your selected missing element.

   COLUMN I

26. Monkey wrenches, 10", jaws open 1 3/4"

27. 25-ft. copper tubing, seamless

28. 5-lbs. rivets, solid steel, button head

29. 2 wrecking bars, goose neck, drop forged steel, 3/4" hexagon

30. 1-gro. screws, wood, flat head, No. 10 x 3/4"

31. Emery cloth, crocus, 9" x 11"

32. 100 ft. rope, 1 inch

   COLUMN II

   A. Length
   B. Quantity
   C. Composition (material)
   D. Diameter

33. If an assistant stockman is performing his work in an unsafe manner, the stockman should IMMEDIATELY   33._____

   A. inform the assistant that if he does not intend to abide by the specific safety rules he should quit
   B. relieve the assistant of his duties and tell him to report to the foreman
   C. stop the assistant and tell him how the job should be done
   D. report the unsafe manner to his foreman

34. It is highly important that damaged items be held intact as received. 34.____
    This is necessary MAINLY in order to

    A. fix responsibility and determine reparations
    B. prevent damaged items being mixed with good items
    C. avoid similar damage on future shipments
    D. ascertain extent of damage

35. An assistant stockman filling a requisition is carrying several lengths of pipe from the 35.____
    rack.
    The MOST serious consequence of carelessness on his part would be a(n)

    A. issue of the wrong length of pipe
    B. error in the entry on the stock card
    C. injury to himself or others
    D. rejection of the lengths offered

36. A stockman instructing a newly appointed stock assistant in the storing of an item not 36.____
    previously stored should place the LEAST emphasis on

    A. time consumed
    B. care required in handling the item
    C. method of piling the item
    D. the location to be used

37. In the interest of safety, it is good practice for storeroom employees to 37.____

    A. wear safety helmets near high shelves
    B. consider the various possibilities of accident on each job
    C. never work alone
    D. check with the foreman before starting any job

38. For BEST storeroom practice, uniform piling of material is desirable because it 38.____

    A. facilitates counting
    B. is the easiest way
    C. presents a good appearance
    D. creates a favorable impression on superiors

39. A stockman receives a complaint from two of his stock assistants that a third stock assis- 39.____
    tant is lazy and fails to do his share of the work.
    The stockman should

    A. reprimand the two assistants for creating discontent
    B. report the accused assistant to the foreman
    C. exercise greater supervision over this assistant
    D. disregard the complaint

40. Occasionally, a stock assistant will resent any checking by the stockman, taking it as a personal matter rather than necessary routine. The BEST way to handle such an assistant is to

   A. ignore him
   B. turn him in for insubordination
   C. assume a much stricter attitude toward him
   D. keep all personal contacts to a minimum

40._____

KEY (CORRECT ANSWERS)

1. A,C	11. C	21. B	31. B
2. D	12. D	22. A	32. C
3. B	13. A	23. C	33. C
4. C	14. D	24. B	34. A
5. B	15. B	25. C	35. C
6. A	16. A	26. B	36. A
7. A	17. B	27. D	37. B
8. D	18. C	28. A,D	38. A
9. C	19. C	29. A	39. C
10. B	20. B	30. C	40. D

TEST 3

DIRECTIONS: Each question or incomplete statement is followed by several suggested answers or completions. Select the one that BEST answers the question or completes the statement. *PRINT THE LETTER OF THE CORRECT ANSWER IN THE SPACE AT THE RIGHT.*

1. A veteran stockman has discovered that some of the material in one of the bins has been misplaced. An investigation discloses that this was due to the carelessness of a newly appointed stock assistant.
   The BEST action for the stockman to take would be to

   A. recommend to the foreman that charges be preferred against the assistant
   B. give the assistant another assignment where accuracy is not essential
   C. impress upon the assistant that he must be more careful
   D. ignore the incident

   1.____

2. Employees of a city agency should regularly read the bulletin board at their job location MAINLY in order to

   A. show that they have an interest in the business of the agency
   B. become familiar with new orders and procedures posted on it
   C. learn what previously posted material has been removed
   D. learn about any changes in the staff of the agency

   2.____

3. A certain drawer will hold 4,000 cards, 6" x 10". The MAXIMUM number of cards of the same thickness, measuring 3" x 5", which the drawer will hold is

   A. 4,000   B. 8,000   C. 12,000   D. 16,000

   3.____

4. The MAIN reason why every accident should be investigated is that

   A. an investigation of a minor accident may uncover a very hazardous condition
   B. the total cost of accidents can then be accurately determined
   C. accurate records can be maintained for insurance purposes
   D. this is the only way to have all accidents reported

   4.____

5. A stock assistant who is continually non-cooperative should

   A. be recommended for a caution
   B. be assigned to undesirable jobs only
   C. never be allowed to work overtime
   D. always be assigned to work alone

   5.____

6. Before turning in a report of an investigation you have made, you discover some additional information you didn't know when writing the report.
   Whether or not to rewrite your report to include this additional information should depend MAINLY on the

   A. bearing this new information will have on the conclusions of the report
   B. number of people who will eventually review the report
   C. number of other reports to be prepared
   D. length of the report

   6.____

7. Assume that one of the stock assistants objects to being constantly assigned to the particularly unpleasant job of sorting scrap material.
   The supervising stockman, insofar as possible, should

   A. rotate him to other jobs
   B. allow him to stop work sooner than the other men
   C. keep him on the assignment and give him an additional assistant
   D. grant him priority on overtime to compensate for this assignment

8. *Men do not stay trained. If they do not forget what they have learned, it is continuously made obsolete by improved technology and social change.*
   The BEST conclusion which can be drawn from this statement is that

   A. most men should not start work until they have completed a training program
   B. training programs should not be concerned with changes in technology
   C. men may have to be retrained after a period of time
   D. training programs are of little value

9. As a responsible stockman, one of the BEST ways of cooperating with your foreman would be to

   A. ask him to decide all problems which may arise
   B. constantly bring to him all the minutest details concerning the storeroom
   C. accept full responsibility for the work assigned to your section by the foreman
   D. constantly bring new ideas to him so that he can determine the advantages and disadvantages

10. The MOST valid reason why a particular job might have a time limit set on it is that

    A. this particular job is urgent
    B. the men will be kept continuously busy
    C. the best quality of work is thus obtained
    D. maximum output can be achieved only in this way

11. A stockman instructing a newly appointed stock assistant in the storing of an item not previously stored should place the LEAST emphasis on

    A. the location to be used
    B. method of piling the item
    C. care required in handling the item
    D. the time required to store the item

12. *Employees must not post or circulate notices or literature of an unauthorized nature on the property of the department.*
    The MOST logical conclusion which can be drawn from this statement is that on department property

    A. politics should not be discussed
    B. newspapers must not be read or passed around
    C. approval would be necessary before posting a political notice
    D. employees may not act in a manner that would cause adverse criticism of the department

13. The time required to fill a requisition will be LEAST affected by the _____ the item requisitioned.

    A. size
    B. location
    C. amount
    D. description

14. The number 0.025 can also be expressed as 25

    A. ten-thousandths
    B. thousandths
    C. hundredths
    D. tenths

15. A stock assistant transporting material through a dimly lighted part of the storeroom dropped one of the articles but continued on his way without picking it up.
    This was poor practice MAINLY because

    A. the article may not be located when needed
    B. someone may trip over the article
    C. it is an indication of carelessness
    D. an erroneous entry may be made on the stock card

16. In opening wooden crates containing glassware, the BEST reason for opening the top first is that

    A. it was nailed on last
    B. the packing slip will be found here
    C. it is easier to remove than any of the other sides
    D. this minimizes the possibility of damage to the contents

17. The decimal which is NEAREST to 27/64 is

    A. 0.418   B. 0.422   C. 0.426   D. 0.430

18. A sledge hammer was requisitioned and later in the day it was returned clean and undamaged to the storeroom.
    On being returned, it would MOST likely be classified as

    A. scrap   B. salvage   C. unused   D. used

19. The result obtained by dividing 36.0 by 0.012 is

    A. 30   B. 300   C. 3,000   D. 30,000

20. A physical inventory is PRIMARILY useful for detecting errors in the

    A. storeroom procedure
    B. perpetual inventory entries
    C. filling of requisitions on stores
    D. processing of requisitions on the purchasing agent

21. A box contains an equal number of aluminum and iron castings. Each iron casting weighs 3 pounds, and each aluminum casting weighs 1 pound.
    If the contents of the box weigh 160 pounds, the total number of castings in the box is

    A. 80   B. 60   C. 40   D. 20

22. To save time in accurately filling requisitions, packaged material should be stored

    A. in adequate bins
    B. in rows of uniform stacks
    C. with the content labels visible
    D. near material with which it is used

23. In the operation of the department, it is always desirable to maintain good public relations.
    The opinion of the public would be LEAST affected by the

    A. attractiveness of subway and bus posters
    B. attitude of the department employees toward the public
    C. cleanliness of the trains and buses
    D. kind of service rendered

24. A shipment of 60 boxes, each containing 1/2 gross of screws, had been received and stored. Several days later, a stockman receives a requisition calling for one gross of round head brass wood screws, No. 4 x 3/4.
    In filling this requisition, it is LEAST essential that he check the

    A. type of head
    B. actual count
    C. diameter of the screws
    D. material of which the screws are made

25. While filling requisitions, you notice that several of a group of crow bars are stored so as to protrude into the aisle.
    Your BEST immediate procedure would be to

    A. store them properly
    B. notify the foreman of the condition
    C. do nothing unless the bars will remain in stock for a considerable time
    D. find the stock assistant who stored the bars and tell him of the dangerous condition

26. The MOST important reason for holding damaged items intact as received is in order to

    A. keep damaged items out of stock
    B. determine the extent of the damage
    C. fix responsibility and determine reparations
    D. determine how to avoid damage on future shipments

27. A certain stock item has not been requisitioned for three years time.
    It can reasonably be assumed that this item is

    A. obsolete   B. over-stocked
    C. worthless   D. valuable

28. Of the following, the MOST important reason why a stockman should be careful when checking incoming stock is that an error made by him may

    A. be costly
    B. never be found
    C. cause a serious delay
    D. set a bad example for the stock assistant

29. An employee, as a basic part of his duties, must notify the office whenever he moves and changes his address. The logical reason for this requirement is to

    A. help the post office, if necessary
    B. prevent the holding of two jobs
    C. enable the authority to contact the employee in time of need
    D. enable the authority to furnish correct information to creditors

30. The BEST of the following reasons why stockmen and assistants are expected to do their work in a definite prescribed manner is that

    A. no other method would work
    B. this is the best way to maintain discipline
    C. good results can be expected with less supervision
    D. this is the fastest possible way to get the work done

31. A department presents to the stockman a requisition which has an obvious error in the stock number.
    The stockman's BEST procedure with the requisition is to

    A. fill the order and ignore the error
    B. destroy all copies and notify his foreman of the incident
    C. correct all copies, issue the stock, and notify the department
    D. point out the error, return the requisition, and have a new, correct one presented

32. Of the following, it is MOST important for a stockman to contact his foreman when

    A. a stock is running low
    B. he thinks the cost of an item is excessive
    C. a foreman personally submits a requisition
    D. he feels that a requisition contains more material than needed

33. *A worker should work a full day every day.*
    This saying means that

    A. a worker should do as much work as he can, as fast as he can
    B. a worker should come to work regularly, on time, and do his job the best way he can
    C. time off for lunch, vacations, and holidays should be cut down as much as possible
    D. it would be better for all businesses to work around-the-clock shifts, seven days a week

34. A stockman receiving a shipment of material notices that it differs from the description on the order.
    He should

    A. reject the shipment
    B. accept the shipment without comment
    C. use another form in place of the MRR
    D. note the difference in the body of the MRR

35. The MOST important of the following reasons for insisting on neatness in the area where stock is distributed is that this

    A. makes for good employee morale
    B. decreases the chances of accidents
    C. prevents tools from becoming rusty
    D. increases the available storage space

36. A shop maintenance gang requisitioned a new 48" pipe wrench while working on a water line. A few days later, the wrench was returned to the storeroom.
    The MRS should indicate the wrench as

    A. salvage   B. scrap   C. used   D. unused

37. In evaluating a stock assistant's services, the stockman would be MOST effectively guided by the man's

    A. present assignment
    B. absenteeism record
    C. general dependability
    D. actions in the stockman's presence

38. Of the sizes given, the FINEST grade of sandpaper is

    A. 00   B. 0   C. 1   D. 2

39. If you are assigned to work with an individual who has many accidents in the storeroom, it would be BEST for you to

    A. refuse to work with this individual
    B. do most of the assigned work yourself
    C. provide this man with a copy of all rules and regulations
    D. personally check the safety precautions in the storeroom

40. A stock assistant asks you what is meant by a number 1/4-20 machine screw. You should tell him that the number 20 indicates only the

    A. type of head
    B. threads per inch
    C. length of the screw
    D. diameter of the screw

KEY (CORRECT ANSWERS)

1. C	11. D	21. A	31. C
2. B	12. C	22. C	32. A
3. D	13. D	23. A	33. B
4. A	14. B	24. B	34. D
5. A	15. B	25. A	35. B
6. A	16. D	26. C	36. C
7. A	17. B	27. A	37. C
8. C	18. C	28. A	38. A
9. C	19. C	29. C	39. D
10. A	20. B	30. C	40. B

TEST 4

DIRECTIONS: Each question or incomplete statement is followed by several suggested answers or completions. Select the one that BEST answers the question or completes the statement. *PRINT THE LETTER OF THE CORRECT ANSWER IN THE SPACE AT THE RIGHT.*

1. If you detect an error in an order issued to you by your foreman, you should FIRST

    A. correct the error yourself and carry out the corrected order
    B. try to carry out the order as issued since that is your job
    C. point out the error to your foreman because it is probably an oversight
    D. put the order aside until your foreman detects and corrects the order himself

2. The MOST important reason for storing material as compact as possible is

    A. to save space
    B. for easy removal
    C. to avoid damage
    D. to prevent stealing

3. It is MOST important for a written report by a stockman to be

    A. accurate as to facts
    B. on department letterhead
    C. properly punctuated
    D. brief

4. Of the following, it is MOST essential to use the first-in, first-out method for material which

    A. moves slowly
    B. may become obsolete
    C. deteriorates with age
    D. is ordered in large quantities

5. When bulletin orders are reissued without change, the purpose is USUALLY to

    A. save time
    B. supersede prior bulletins
    C. make sure the order reaches all bulletin boards
    D. remind employees that the order is still important

6. If your boss tells you that, in general, your work is good, but there is one job he would like to see you do better, you should

    A. avoid that one job from now on
    B. tell him that he is not perfect either
    C. ask him to pick someone else to do that job
    D. tell him that you will try to do that job better in the future

7. The number of sheets in a ream of paper is

    A. 250   B. 500   C. 750   D. 1000

8. In standard report forms, it is advisable to print rather than write in the entries because printing generally

    A. looks better
    B. is more legible
    C. is easier to do
    D. occupies less space

9. The last entry on a card containing a perpetual inventory of material should show the total amount of this material

   A. disbursed
   B. received
   C. in stock
   D. on order

10. Assume that a stockman notices a man standing in a store-room and suspects from the man's actions that he may have no business being there.
    The MOST reasonable procedure would be for the stockman to

    A. call the transit police
    B. ignore him and continue to work
    C. immediately order the man out of the storeroom
    D. ask the man what business he has being there

11. When a storing procedure of long standing is changed, it is desirable that detailed instructions thereon be issued in writing rather than given verbally.
    The reason for using written instructions is that they

    A. can be printed in quantity and replaced if lost
    B. can be repeatedly reviewed
    C. are more easily understood
    D. carry more weight

12. In a shipment of 12 castings, there were 2 defective pieces which were rejected by the inspector.
    These rejected pieces should be reported on the form known as a

    A. shipping memorandum
    B. DCR
    C. MRR
    D. MRS

13. The rules state that employees should not make any statements concerning any accidents except to proper officials of the department.
    The PROBABLE reason for this rule is to

    A. prevent lawsuits
    B. avoid conflicting testimony
    C. conceal facts which may be damaging to the department
    D. prevent unofficial statements from being accepted as official

14. In assigning a suitable place in the stock room for storing a particular item, the LEAST important factor to consider is

    A. its size
    B. its fragility
    C. the frequency of requests for it
    D. the importance of the sections using it

15. The MAIN reason for not permitting more than one person to work on a ladder at the same time is that

    A. the ladder might get overloaded
    B. time would be lost going up and down the ladder
    C. several persons on the ladder might obstruct each other
    D. several persons could not all face the ladder at one time

16. You have been assigned to a job and told that it has to be finished by a certain time. If, after working for some time, you realize that you cannot finish the job on time, you should

    A. notify your boss immediately of this situation
    B. skip what you consider to be minor parts of the job
    C. continue working and get as much done as possible
    D. complain to your boss that you are being overworked

17. Upon being assigned to a stockroom where he had not worked before, it is essential that the stockman be made thoroughly acquainted with the stockroom layout PRIMARILY to

    A. store items safely
    B. make changes in bin and shelf locations
    C. facilitate his handling of materials
    D. be able to suggest improvements in storing methods

18. If it is necessary to determine the number of large bolts loosely filling a large barrel without making a total count, the BEST procedure is to

    A. count one-tenth of the barrel and multiply by 10
    B. measure one bolt and measure the volume of the barrel
    C. count a small box full and measure the rest with the box
    D. weigh a few, weigh the barrel, weigh a similar empty barrel

19. When carrying pipes, employees are cautioned against lifting with the fingers inserted in the ends.
    The PROBABLE reason for this caution is to avoid the possibility of

    A. straining finger muscles
    B. dropping and damaging pipe
    C. cutting fingers on the edge of the pipe
    D. getting dirt and perspiration on the inside of the pipe

20. Discarded metal is returned to stores and handled as scrap rather than thrown in with other debris because

    A. of its potential value
    B. it cannot be as easily disposed of
    C. it weighs more than the other debris
    D. of the possibility of causing an accident

21. The MAIN purpose of giving some employees instructions in first aid is to

    A. reduce the number of accidents
    B. save money on compensation cases
    C. eliminate the need for calling doctors
    D. be able to provide emergency aid if needed

22. Fire extinguishers are provided in storerooms to be used in case of fire. To make sure that these extinguishers are always in readiness, they should be periodically

    A. rotated   B. replaced
    C. inspected   D. used

23. When a department first-aid kit is opened, it is NOT necessary to report the 23.____

   A. kind of injury involved
   B. amount of each material used
   C. name of the person for whom the kit was opened
   D. last previous date on which the kit was opened

24. A newly assigned stockman is MOST likely to secure the respect of his assistants if he 24.____

   A. doesn't push the men too hard
   B. shows a thorough knowledge of his job
   C. overlooks minor infractions of rules
   D. fraternizes with them after hours

25. If you and another stockman are assigned to a hard and tedious job and your co-worker is not doing a reasonable share of the work, your BEST procedure is to 25.____

   A. slow down your rate
   B. do your share and quit
   C. try to persuade him to do his share
   D. register a complaint with your boss before continuing

26. The first thing which a stock assistant should do after receiving a requisition for an item which is NOT in stock is to 26.____

   A. look for a comparable item to substitute
   B. file the requisition until the item is in stock
   C. investigate to determine if the item is on order
   D. inform the person making the requisition that the item will be in stock

27. For BEST storeroom practice, uniform piling of material is desirable because it 27.____

   A. is the easiest way to store material
   B. makes counting easier
   C. presents a good appearance
   D. creates a favorable impression on superiors

28. A stockman receives a complaint from two of his stock assistants that a third stock assistant is lazy and fails to do his share of the work.
The stockman should 28.____

   A. disregard the complaint
   B. exercise greater supervision over this assistant
   C. reprimand the two assistants for creating discontent
   D. report this assistant to the foreman

29. When deciding upon storage space for items of an inflammable nature, it is DESIRABLE to 29.____

   A. avoid cross ventilation   B. use only a small space
   C. avoid a damp location   D. use an isolated area

30. A contributing cause present in practically ALL accidents is

    A. use of improper tools
    B. lack of cooperation among the men in the gang
    C. failure to give close attention to the job at hand
    D. failure to place the right man in the right job

31. The MOST important reason for the requirement that every city department operate within a budget is that a budget will

    A. establish a good base for comparing this year's activities with last year's
    B. enable a department to cut down on provisional appointments
    C. clearly define the area of responsibility of a department
    D. enable spending to be controlled in advance

32. Carelessness on the part of a stock assistant generally can NOT be overcome by

    A. stricter discipline
    B. closer supervision
    C. more thorough training
    D. less difficult assignments

33. A report of an unusual occurrence is MOST likely to be accurate as to facts if written by the stockman

    A. briefly
    B. at considerable length
    C. right after the occurrence
    D. after discussion with his boss

34. Of the following, the job that is BEST for a stockman to delegate to one of the stock assistants is one that

    A. occupies the greatest percentage of his time
    B. is of a policy-making nature
    C. he finds disagreeable
    D. is routine

35. The LEAST effective way for you to train a newly appointed stock assistant is to

    A. let him watch you do the job until he becomes expert
    B. let him do a job he has never done, under your close supervision
    C. let him make mistakes so that he will remember better
    D. explain the job to him orally

36. A foreman should impress upon the men under his supervision to report every unsafe condition which they may notice.
    The MOST important action resulting from such a report is that each unsafe condition will be

    A. recorded   B. corrected
    C. investigated   D. satisfactorily explained

37. Certain items received by a storeroom are not put in stock until they have been accepted by the using department's inspector.
   The MOST logical reason for this procedure is that

   A. due to long time between ordering and delivery, these items may no longer be needed
   B. these items are frequently damaged in transit
   C. the items received may be of an inferior quality
   D. there may be a shortage in the number of items received

37.____

38. An orientation program for a group of new men should NOT ordinarily include

   A. a statement of the rules pertaining to sick leave, vacation, holidays, etc.
   B. a brief description of the physical layout of the shop
   C. detailed instructions on the job of each man
   D. a brief review of the organization chart

38.____

39. A full reel of cable weighs 1170 pounds. If the empty reel weighs 225 pounds and the cable weighs 6.43 pounds per foot, the number of feet of cable on the full reel is MOST NEARLY

   A. 141   B. 144   C. 147   D. 150

39.____

40. The frequency with which reports are submitted should depend MAINLY on

   A. the importance of changes in the information included in the report
   B. the availability of an experienced man to write the report
   C. how comprehensive the report has to be
   D. the amount of information in the report

40.____

KEY (CORRECT ANSWERS)

1. C	11. B	21. D	31. D
2. A	12. C	22. C	32. D
3. A	13. D	23. D	33. C
4. C	14. D	24. B	34. D
5. D	15. A	25. C	35. C
6. D	16. A	26. C	36. B
7. B	17. C	27. B	37. C
8. B	18. D	28. B	38. C
9. C	19. C	29. D	39. C
10. D	20. A	30. C	40. A

EXAMINATION SECTION
TEST 1

DIRECTIONS: Each question or incomplete statement is followed by several suggested answers or completions. Select the one that BEST answers the question or completes the statement. *PRINT THE LETTER OF THE CORRECT ANSWER IN THE SPACE AT THE RIGHT.*

Questions 1-10.

DIRECTIONS: Questions 1 through 10 are to be answered on the basis of Tables I and II below.

TABLE I
Building 5 Storeroom
Report of Dollar Cost of Stores Issued To
All Divisions in the Month of December

Divisions	11 Dept. Reports & Bulletins	12 Food Supplies	13 Motor Vehicle Supplies	14 Office Supplies	15 Printed Stationery & Forms	16 Printing & Reproducing Supplies	17 Small Tools & Implements
A	40		125	85	13	55	45
B	21		231	35	46	32	61
C	68	422		75	37	81	
D	81			83	98	77	91
E	32	168		69	51	43	

TABLE II
Building 5 Storeroom

Summary of Dollar Cost of Stores Issued
and Received and Balances, December

1 Supply Code	2 Balance Beginning of Month	3 Receipts From Vendors	4 Receipts From Storehouse A	5 Receipts From Storehouse B	6 Total Receipts	7 Total Issued	8 Balance
11	200	112	83	21	216	242	174
12	472	225	200	46	471	590	119
13	365	400			765	356	409
14	257	75	245	27	347	357	
15	245	89	152	36	277	255	277
16	281	104	190		294	288	287
17	197	32	110	40	182	197	182

1. The average value of small tools and implements received by Division C and E during the month of December

   A. is zero
   B. is approximately 78
   C. is 197
   D. cannot be determined from the information given

2. The division which received the GREATEST dollar value of stores in the month of December was

   A. A   B. B   C. C   D. D

3. The division which received the GREATEST number of items in all supply categories in December

   A. is A
   B. is B
   C. is D
   D. cannot be determined from the information given

4. In the column *Total Issued,* the entry which is INCORRECT is for

   A. Food Supplies
   B. Motor Vehicle Supplies
   C. Office Supplies
   D. Printed Stationery & Forms

5. In the column *Total Receipts,* the entry which is INCORRECT is for

   A. Department Reports & Bulletins
   B. Motor Vehicle Supplies
   C. Office Supplies
   D. Small Tools & Equipment

6. The Balance for Supply Code 14 has been omitted. This figure should be

   A. 10   B. 247   C. 367   D. 594

7. The Balance has been INCORRECTLY entered for

   A. Department Reports and Bulletins
   B. Food Supplies
   C. Printing and Reproducing Supplies
   D. Small Tools and Equipment

8. The dollar value of department reports and bulletins received from vendors in December exceeds that received from the storehouses by

   A. 8   B. 12
   C. 29   D. an indeterminate amount

9. For the classes of items received from Storehouse B during the month of December, the average dollar cost of these classes was MOST NEARLY

   A. 24   B. 34   C. 65   D. 170

10. One space is left blank in Column 4 of Table II. Judging only from the above tables, the MOST probable reason for this is that 10.____

   A. motor vehicle supplies were obtained from vendors only
   B. number 365 was inadvertently omitted from Column 4
   C. the figures for Columns 4 and 5 were included in Column 3
   D. the motor vehicle supply stock of Storehouse A is below the minimum stock level

11. If a physical inventory reveals a much smaller number of a particular item than is shown by the perpetual inventory record, it PROBABLY indicates 11.____

   A. a discontinuation of the stocking of the item
   B. a failure to record a withdrawal on the inventory record
   C. an unusual consumption of that particular item
   D. the non-delivery of an order for that item

12. The number of cartons measuring 3' x 3' x 2' which will be needed to pack 1,728 boxed items each measuring 12.____
    3" x 9" x 6" is

   A. 9   B. 18   C. 108   D. 192

13. Assume that a storehouse floor is 300 feet long, 200 feet wide, and 10 feet high. The total weight that the floor can hold is 3,000 tons. 13.____
    The safe floor load is _____ pounds per square foot.

   A. 100   B. 200   C. 300   D. 600

14. Seventy cartons, each 2 feet wide, 3 feet long, and 4 feet high, will require storage space measuring APPROXIMATELY _____ cubic yards. 14.____

   A. 24   B. 56   C. 63   D. 187

15. A certain item is stored in a crate measuring 3 feet in length, 4 feet in width, and 6 inches in height. It weighs 60 pounds. 15.____
    If the usable height of the storage area is twelve feet and if the safe floor load is 140 pounds per square foot, the number of crates which may be stacked right side up in a single column is

   A. 2   B. 5   C. 11   D. 24

16. You have to load 5,000 items on trucks each having a maximum load capacity of 2 1/2 tons. Each item weighs 20 pounds and takes up 2 cubic feet of storage space. Assume that the storage space in each truck has an area of 68 square feet and is 6 feet high. Without exceeding space or weight limitations, the SMALLEST number of trucks that could be used is 16.____

   A. 20   B. 25   C. 50   D. 63

17. Twenty pallet loads of a certain commodity have to be unloaded from a truck and moved to a certain location in the storehouse. It takes a forklift truck five minutes to unload two pallet loads at one time and place them on a trailer which can hold four pallet loads. It takes one tractor ten minutes to move five loaded trailers to the proper location in the storehouse.
Using one forklift truck, one tractor, and five trailers, and assuming no other time lost, the pallet loads can be unloaded and moved to the place where they will be stacked in

    A. 50 minutes B. 60 minutes
    C. 90 minutes D. 2 hours

17.____

18. A storeroom is 100 feet long and 26 feet wide. One aisle 8 feet wide runs the length of the storeroom. One aisle 4 feet wide runs the width of the storeroom.
If there were no other aisles, the number of square feet of usable storage space would be

    A. 1,696 B. 1,728 C. 2,280 D. 2,568

18.____

19. A discount of 1% is given on all purchases of a certain item in quantities of 100 units or more. An additional discount of 1% is given on that portion of the purchase which exceeds 300.
If 450 units are purchased at a list price of $6.00, the total cost is

    A. $2,619 B. $2,664 C. $2,670 D. $2,682

19.____

20. The amount of turpentine on hand is 271/2 gallons. One requisition is filled for 3 1/4 gallons, two additional requisitions are filled for 1 quart 8 ounces each, and five requisitions are filled for 2 pints 2 ounces each. The quantity of turpentine remaining after all these requisitions have been filled is

    A. 20 gal. 3 qts. 1 pt.   B. 21 gal. 3 qts. 1 pt.
    C. 22 gal. 1 qt. 6 oz.   D. 22 gal. 1 1/2 qts. 10 oz.

20.____

21. If the average height of the stacks in your section of the storehouse is 9 1/2 feet, the area which will be occupied by 11,400 cubic feet of supplies is APPROXIMATELY _____ square feet.

    A. 100 B. 120 C. 1,000 D. 1,200

21.____

22. Letting oily rags or dust cloths accumulate in a closet is a fire hazard PRINCIPALLY because of the possibility of

    A. a match or cigarette being dropped
    B. fire spreading from other areas
    C. spontaneous combustion
    D. their use in inflammable areas

22.____

23. Assume that you have depleted your entire stock of 1,692 units of a certain item by sending 524 units to one location and dividing the remainder of the stock equally among 16 other locations.
The number of units that was sent to each of these 16 locations was

    A. 48 B. 73 C. 116 D. 168

23.____

24. Of the following, the MOST advisable way to increase storage space is to
    A. decrease stock supplies below minimum
    B. eliminate items that are infrequently used
    C. stack to maximum height
    D. utilize aisle space

25. In a large storehouse, an area with a high ceiling is ordinarily BEST for storing items which are
    A. irregular in shape, heavy, and on skids
    B. irregular in shape, light, and on pallets
    C. rectangular in shape and on pallets
    D. rectangular in shape and on skids

26. The term *legal-size* refers to paper which is generally _____ than letter-size paper.
    A. longer
    B. longer and narrower
    C. longer and wider
    D. wider

27. A *trier* is a device used for
    A. sampling   B. sealing   C. stamping   D. weighing

28. Of the following items, the one for which the MOST care should be taken to prevent moth damage is
    A. nylon brushes
    B. orlon fabrics
    C. pianos
    D. shoes

29. Circulation of air is LEAST desirable for
    A. batteries   B. cement   C. linoleum   D. paint

30. There are five units of a circular piece of equipment which weighs 9,000 pounds and has a solid circular base and a solid circular top each 4 feet in diameter.
    In MOST cases, the BEST way to store these five units would be to
    A. crate them and place one next to the other
    B. crate them and stack them two high
    C. place one next to the other without crating
    D. stack them two high without crating

31. You have just received a shipment of 500 packages, each 2" long, 1' wide, and 1/2' high, and each weighing 25 pounds. You are going to store them in an area 10' by 10' by 10' where the safe floor load is 100 pounds per square foot. The number of these packages which may be safely stored right side up is
    A. 100   B. 200   C. 400   D. 500

32. Assume that you have several men and the following equipment available: two forklift trucks, one tractor, five trailers, and two handtrucks.
    In order to move twenty pallet loads 200 yards in a storehouse, it would be MOST advisable for you to use the

A. forklift trucks
B. tractor and the trailers
C. tractor, the trailers, and the forklift trucks
D. tractor, the trailers, the handtrucks, and one fork-lift truck

33. Of the following, the MOST suitable temperature for the storage of fresh milk is

    A. 0° F B. 16° F C. 32° F D. 48° F

34. Of the following, the MOST suitable temperature for the storage of frozen meats is

    A. 0° F B. 16° F C. 32° F D. 48° F

35. An isolated section of the storehouse has just been made available for your use. It has all the facilities available in other sections of the storehouse, except that it is distant from shipping and receiving areas and all centers of activity.
Of the following items in the storehouse, the one which should ordinarily receive priority consideration for storage in such a section is

    A. codeine B. flour C. gasoline D. machinery

36. Assume that you have to move 100 pallets from one location in the warehouse to another about 20 feet away. Which of the following would you need to do the job MOST efficiently?

    A. Conveyor
    B. Forklift truck
    C. Forklift truck, tractor, trailers
    D. Four-wheel handtruck, portable elevator

37. Of the following, the QUICKEST and EASIEST way to move thirty pallet loads of material 800 feet and then stack then is to use a

    A. forklift truck and a tractor-trailer train
    B. forklift truck and a crane
    C. portable elevator
    D. portable elevator and 6 handtrucks

38. The BEST measure of the effectiveness of a tractor-trailer combination is the

    A. amount of power used per day
    B. amount of stock that can be moved in a day
    C. amount of stock that can be moved in each trip
    D. number of miles which can be covered in a day

39. As compared to a conventional counterbalance design fork-lift truck, a straddle arm fork-lift truck with the same lifting capacity will USUALLY weigh

    A. approximately the same   B. less
    C. much more   D. slightly more

40. The one of the following which is NOT of major importance in determining the location of an item in a storehouse is

    A. difficulty of handling   B. fire hazard
    C. floor strength   D. purpose for which used

41. A usually competent stockman under your supervision has complained to you that a newly employed assistant stockman knows nothing about handling or storing stock.
Of the following, the MOST advisable course of action for you to take is to

   A. advise the stockman not to interfere
   B. arrange for a transfer of the new worker
   C. ask the stockman whether he is willing to assist in on-the-job training
   D. tell the new worker that he will have to do better

41.____

42. Assume that an employee tells you that you have made an error in issuing certain instructions. You do not believe this to be true.
The MOST appropriate action for you to take in MOST cases is to

   A. ask him to follow the instructions as they were given
   B. get some of the other employees together to discuss the matter
   C. have him explain why he believes it to be an error
   D. tell him to do it any way he wants to, as long as the job gets done

42.____

43. In planning a large operation involving the movement and handling of stock, it would be MOST desirable for a storekeeper to

   A. confer only with his supervisor and other storekeepers
   B. discuss the matter only with his more capable subordinates
   C. have his subordinates participate in the planning
   D. rely solely upon his own judgment and knowledge

43.____

44. As a storekeeper, you find that routine and clerical duties greatly decrease the time you can spend in supervising your subordinates.
Of the following, you should FIRST attempt to

   A. delegate some of your supervisory duties to the most qualified subordinates
   B. have an assistant assigned to take over some of your duties
   C. reduce the number of persons under your supervision
   D. turn over some of the routine and clerical work to your subordinates

44.____

45. As a storekeeper in charge of a storehouse, you find that there is a considerable backlog in the filling of requisitions, and you have received complaints from using agencies Of the following, the MOST advisable course of action for you to take FIRST is to

   A. advise the using agencies that they must wait their turn
   B. determine the factors causing the backlog
   C. take appropriate disciplinary action where indicated
   D. work out plans for removing the backlog

45.____

46. It is necessary for you to assign one of the men in the storehouse to the main office for two weeks to work on records.
Which of the following men should be chosen?

   A. Al is the best at records work, but he is very reluctant to go.
   B. Ben is next to Al in ability of records work and is interested in going, but he is so likeable that you are afraid the main office will want to keep him permanently.

46.____

C. Carl is next to Ben in ability at records work, but it would be a great hardship for him to go because of his time schedule and the traveling.
D. Dan has little ability at records work, but he has not done well in your division and he is anxious to try working in the main office.

47. An employee under your supervision comes to you to complain about an assignment you have made. You consider the matter to be unimportant, but it seems to be very important to him. He is excited and very angry.
Of the following, the MOST advisable action to take FIRST is to

   A. let him talk until he *gets it off his chest*
   B. refuse to talk to him until he has *cooled down*
   C. show him at once how unimportant the matter is
   D. tell him to talk it over with the other employees

48. Of the following, the BEST reason why accuracy in keeping records should be considered more important than speed is that

   A. most employees cannot work rapidly and also be accurate
   B. most supervisors insist upon accurate work, while very few pay attention to speed
   C. much time may be lost correcting or redoing work that is done too hastily
   D. speedy workers are usually inaccurate

49. A fistfight develops between two stockmen under your supervision.
The MOST advisable course of action for you to take FIRST is to

   A. call the police
   B. have the other workers pull them apart
   C. order them to stop
   D. step between the two men

50. You have assigned some difficult and unusual work to one of your most experienced and competent subordinates.
If you notice that he is doing the work incorrectly, you should

   A. assign the work to another employee
   B. reprimand him in private
   C. show him immediately how the work should be done
   D. wait until the job is completed and then correct his errors

KEY (CORRECT ANSWERS)

1. A	11. B	21. D	31. D	41. C
2. C	12. A	22. C	32. A	42. C
3. D	13. A	23. B	33. C	43. C
4. D	14. C	24. C	34. A	44. D
5. B	15. D	25. C	35. C	45. B
6. B	16. B	26. A	36. B	46. B
7. B	17. B	27. A	37. A	47. A
8. A	18. B	28. C	38. B	48. C
9. B	19. B	29. B	39. B	49. C
10. A	20. C	30. C	40. D	50. C

EXAMINATION SECTION
TEST 1

DIRECTIONS: Each question or incomplete statement is followed by several suggested answers or completions. Select the one that BEST answers the question or completes the statement. *PRINT THE LETTER OF THE CORRECT ANSWER IN THE SPACE AT THE RIGHT.*

1. Of the following, the MOST probable hazard in storing subsistence supplies, such as meats and cereal products, is   1.____

    A. breakage
    B. flammability
    C. spillage
    D. spoilage

2. Of the following, the one which is usually LEAST likely to be shown on properly maintained bin tags is the   2.____

    A. amount received
    B. amount withdrawn
    C. anticipated yearly need
    D. balance on hand

3. Use of materials handling equipment rather than man-power for handling heavy loads generally results in   3.____

    A. increased danger of back injuries
    B. increased productivity
    C. reduction of the height of piled materials
    D. reduced productivity

4. When reviewing the operations of a storage facility, of the following, it is LEAST important that the storekeeper review the   4.____

    A. safety standards being followed
    B. utilization of space for storage
    C. accuracy of storage records
    D. prices used in the preparation of purchase orders

5. A storekeeper in charge of a storehouse has a practice of issuing to only one or two employees the key to the security room where small items of very high dollar value are stored.
   This practice is generally   5.____

    A. *desirable;* it prevents items of small value from being placed in the security room
    B. *desirable;* it helps to fix responsibility for safeguarding the items in the security room
    C. *undesirable;* not even the storekeeper in charge should have a key to the security room of a storehouse
    D. *undesirable;* each employee of the storehouse should have a key to the security room

6. A basic reason for assigning commodity code numbers to purchased and stored items is to   6.____

    A. prevent pilferage
    B. increase the use of mechanized equipment

47

C. facilitate ready reference in communications
D. decrease flexibility of storage areas

7. Of the following, a well-managed storage operation is MOST likely to reduce the

   A. coordination between purchasing and stores operations
   B. idle time of operating personnel awaiting material
   C. turnover of stored materials
   D. utilization of mechanical aids

7.____

8. Which of the following is NOT an important reason for authorizing a purchasing department to control stores?

   A. Coordination of purchasing and stores may result in economies.
   B. Record keeping of materials in storage is closely associated with the purchase of materials.
   C. The storage division can inform purchasing of turnover of items to prevent overstocking or understocking.
   D. The storerooms will be near the points of use, reducing transportation costs.

8.____

9. Of the following, the MOST important daily maintenance requirement for electric forklift trucks is usually

   A. charging the batteries
   B. checking tire pressure
   C. greasing all fittings
   D. tightening the chain link belt of the lift

9.____

10. Generally, it is considered desirable practice to maintain stock at a three-months level of supply.
    Under what circumstances would it be MOST desirable to reduce stock levels to a one-month period?

    A. Discounts when buying larger quantities
    B. Few obsolete items
    C. Rapid deterioration of items
    D. Rising prices

10.____

11. The BEST pallet to use for transporting pallet unit loads in motor freight trucks and railroad cars is generally the _____ pallet.

    A. standard skid   B. straddle truck type
    C. 4-way entry   D. 2-way entry

11.____

12. You find that delivery of a certain item cannot possibly be made to a using agency by the date the using agency requested.
    Of the following, the MOST advisable course of action for you to take FIRST is to

    A. cancel the order and inform the using agency
    B. discuss the problem with the using agency
    C. notify the using agency to obtain the item through direct purchase
    D. schedule the delivery for the earliest possible date

12.____

13. In storing items such as batteries, twine, wire, baled textiles, and other commodities subject to damage or compression by weight, the MOST efficient means of storage is by use of

    A. bin type storage racks
    B. metal containers
    C. pallet adapters
    D. pinwheel stacks

14. Where a lateral haul of 600 feet is required to transport large quantities of pipe stock, the BEST equipment to use is a

    A. forklift truck
    B. gravity-roller conveyor
    C. stock selector truck
    D. tractor and trailers

15. One hundred cartons of paper towels are to be unloaded from a truck to the receiving platform. The floor of the truck is three feet above the platform.
    Of the following, the one that is MOST suitable to use for this purpose is a

    A. forklift truck
    B. four-wheel platform handtruck
    C. gravity conveyor
    D. hand-operated electric skid truck

16. The BEST of the following reasons for developing understudies to storehouse supervisory staff is that this practice

    A. assures that capable staff will not leave their jobs since they are certain to be promoted
    B. helps to assure continued efficiency in a storehouse when persons in important positions leave their jobs
    C. improves morale by demonstrating to employees the opportunities for advancement
    D. provides an opportunity for giving on-the-job training

17. It is said that the morale of a staff is usually a good indication of the quality of leadership exercised by the supervisor of the staff.
    Of the following, the BEST indication of high morale among a staff is:

    A. Disciplinary actions against members of the staff are rare
    B. It is seldom necessary for the staff to work overtime
    C. The staff is seldom late in reporting for work
    D. The staff subordinates personal desires in favor of group objectives

18. The primary responsibility of a supervisor is to

    A. gain the confidence and make friends of all his subordinates
    B. get the work done properly
    C. satisfy his superior and gain his respect
    D. train the men in new methods for doing the work

19. Of the following, the MOST important value of a manual of procedures is that it usually

    A. eliminates the need for on-the-job training
    B. decreases the span of control which can be exercised by individual supervisory personnel
    C. outlines methods of operation for ready reference
    D. provides concrete examples of work previously performed by employees

20. Reprimanding a subordinate when he has done something wrong should be done primarily in order to

    A. deter others from similar acts
    B. improve the subordinate's future performance
    C. maintain discipline
    D. uphold departmental rules

21. Assume that one of the three units in a storehouse under your supervision has developed a considerable backlog of unfilled orders, whereas the other two are up-to-date. The one of the following measures which it would usually be MOST desirable to take in order to reduce this backlog immediately is to

    A. do a study to increase the efficiency of the unit with the backlog of unfilled orders
    B. establish a deadline by which date the unit with the backlog of unfilled orders must complete all of its work
    C. establish an ordered overtime work schedule for the unit with the backlog of unfilled orders
    D. reassign on a temporary basis some workers from the other two units to the unit with the backlog of unfilled orders

22. The success of a program for training employees for current job competence may normally be measured BEST by the

    A. amount of enthusiasm displayed by the participants during the program
    B. extent to which the course content is used in daily operations
    C. length of time that the subject matter of the program is retained
    D. speed with which the subject matter of the program is learned

23. Of the following, the primary consideration in determining the number of people which one individual can supervise is the

    A. amount of time the individual can devote to supervision
    B. individual's knowledge of the work performed by the persons being supervised
    C. nature and variety of activities performed by the persons being supervised
    D. place where the work is performed

24. Assume that you, a storekeeper in charge of a warehouse section, have been considering making changes in the procedures to be followed in your section.
While you are engaged in making this study, and in order to gain acceptance for any changes you might propose as a result of this study, it is generally MOST advisable for you to get comments and recommendations from

A. professional staff of the organization and planning unit of your department
B. storekeepers in charge of other sections of the warehouse who have made changes in their own sections
C. your subordinates who might be affected by any changes
D. your superior

25. Of the following positions, the one for which you may expect normally to have the greatest amount of difficulty in determining meaningful numerical work standards is a(n) 25.____

   A. forklift operator
   B. inventory clerk
   C. order picker
   D. watchman

KEY (CORRECT ANSWERS)

1. D
2. C
3. B
4. D
5. B

6. C
7. B
8. D
9. A
10. C

11. C
12. B
13. C
14. D
15. C

16. B
17. D
18. B
19. C
20. B

21. D
22. B
23. C
24. C
25. D

TEST 2

DIRECTIONS: Each question or incomplete statement is followed by several suggested answers or completions. Select the one that BEST answers the question or completes the statement. *PRINT THE LETTER OF THE CORRECT ANSWER IN THE SPACE AT THE RIGHT.*

1. In teaching new employees how to use forklift equipment, the BEST procedure to follow is:

    A. Give class lecture instructions and then let the employees use the equipment
    B. Let the employees try it themselves and then show them what they are doing wrong
    C. Show the employees how you use the equipment and then answer any questions they may have
    D. Tell the employees how to do it, give a demonstration, have the employees do it, and correct their mistakes

    1.____

2. Assume that you have assigned one of your assistant stockmen to perform a task involving several steps that he has never done before.
   In this situation, of the following, it is generally MOST important for you to

    A. check closely each step in the task as it is being performed or immediately after its completion
    B. make sure that the assistant stockman fully understands the last step before he starts the task
    C. make available to the assistant stockman any tools and equipment that he may request
    D. stress the importance of the task to the assistant stockman

    2.____

3. On the first morning that you report to work at a new job location as a newly-promoted supervisor of a small unit, your superior asks you what you would like to do FIRST.
   Of the following, the LEAST appropriate response for you to make is to say, *I'd like to*

    A. *meet the employees who work in my unit*
    B. *recommend some changes in the procedures used in my unit*
    C. *obtain a manual of procedure, if one is available.*
    D. *see the physical area in which my unit works*

    3.____

4. Assume that a storekeeper has assigned a laborer to assist a stockman in doing a certain task. The stockman reports to the storekeeper that the laborer has not been doing the work which he, the stockman, has been assigning him.
   The MOST appropriate action for the storekeeper to take FIRST in this situation is to

    A. direct the laborer to obey the instructions of the stockman
    B. have a conference with both the stockman and the laborer present
    C. reassign the laborer to another task
    D. speak to the laborer to get his side of the story

    4.____

5. Assume that you have received a delivery of sand, which took up the entire area of a trailer with interior dimensions of 40 feet by 7 feet, and the sand was loaded to an average depth of 4 feet.
   The amount of storage space, in cubic yards, required for this shipment of sand is MOST NEARLY _____ cubic yards.

   A. 42   B. 125   C. 374   D. 1,120

6. Assume that lubricating oil is delivered to your warehouse in 20 gallon drums. Requisitions for amounts less than 20 gallons are filled by drawing off the required amount of lubricating oil from one of the 20 gallon drums. After filling several requisitions for various amounts of lubricating oil, you find that you have on hand 18 full drums, 6 drums that are three-quarters full, 4 drums that are one-half full, and 8 drums that are one-quarter full.
   The total amount of lubricating oil that you have on hand is _____ gallons.

   A. 360   B. 530   C. 540   D. 600

7. Assume that your warehouse issues paint in gallon cans and in quart cans. At the beginning of a certain week, you have 150 gallon cans and 100 quart cans of paint on hand. On Monday, you issue 10 gallon cans and 9 quart cans; on Tuesday, 9 gallon cans and 4 quart cans; on Wednesday, 4 gallon cans and 7 quart cans; on Thursday, 7 gallon cans and 11 quart cans; and on Friday, you issue 5 gallon cans and 5 quart cans.
   The total number of cans of paint on hand at the end of this week, assuming you have received no shipments of paint, is _____ gallon cans and _____ quart cans.

   A. 35; 36   B. 65; 64   C. 65; 86   D. 115; 64

8. A storage carton with dimensions of 1 foot 6 inches by 2 feet 4 inches by 4 feet has MOST NEARLY a volume of _____ cubic feet.

   A. 9.33   B. 10   C. 14   D. 15.36

9. Assume that you can purchase a gallon of turpentine for $1.70. A discount of 10% is given for purchases of 80 gallons or more.
   If you purchase 100 gallons of turpentine, the unit cost of one QUART is MOST NEARLY _____ cents.

   A. 38   B. 43   C. 77   D. 85

10. Assume that you have dispatched a truck at 9 A.M. to make a single delivery at a location which is 20 miles from your warehouse.
    Assuming that the truck travels at an average speed of 15 miles per hour and that one-half hour is required to make the delivery, you should expect the truck to return to the warehouse at approximately

    A. 10:50 A.M.   B. 11:40 A.M.
    C. 12:10 P.M.   D. 12:40 P.M.

11. Assume that you are informed that on the next day at 9 A.M. you will receive six truckloads of goods. Two man-hours are required to unload each truckload of goods, and 6 man-hours are required to place each truckload of goods in storage.
    If you plan to complete this task by 1 P.M., the MINIMUM number of men that you should assign to this task is

    A. 4   B. 8   C. 12   D. 16

12. Assume that you have in stock 15 one-gallon cans of rubber cement thinner.
After filling an order for 50 bottles each containing 16 fluid ounces of rubber cement thinner, the amount of rubber cement thinner remaining in stock is

    A. none; you do not have enough stock to fill this order
    B. 1 gallon 1 quart
    C. 4 gallons 1 1/2 quarts
    D. 8 gallons 3 quarts

13. Assume that you have been instructed to order mineral spirits as soon as the supply on hand falls to the level required for sixty days of issue.
If the total amount of mineral spirits on hand is 960 gallons and you issue an average of 8 gallons of mineral spirits per day, and your warehouse works a five-day week, you will be required to order mineral spirits in _____ working days.

    A. 50   B. 60   C. 70   D. 80

Questions 14-17.

DIRECTIONS: Questions 14 through 17 are to be answered SOLELY or the basis of the information given below.

NUMBER OF SPECIAL ORDERS PICKED AND PACKED EACH DAY DURING. WEEK

Stockman A - Monday 20; Tuesday 20; Wednesday 25;
    Thursday 30; Friday 30

Stockman B - Monday 25; Tuesday 30; Wednesday 35;
    Thursday 20; Friday 35

Stockman C - Monday 15; Tuesday 20; Wednesday 25;
    Thursday 30; Friday 30

Stockman D - Monday 30; Tuesday 35; Wednesday 40;
    Thursday 35; Friday 40

14. Which stockman picked and packed a total of exactly 120 special orders during the week?
Stockman

    A. A   B. B   C. C   D. D

15. The stockman who picked and packed the LEAST number of special orders on Thursday is Stockman

    A. A   B. B   C. C   D. D

16. The total number of special orders picked and packed during the week by all four stockmen is

    A. 125   B. 460   C. 560   D. 570

17. By what percentage did the number of orders picked and packed by Stockman C on Friday exceed the number of orders picked and packed by Stockman C on Monday?

    A. 15%   B. 30%   C. 100%   D. 200%

Questions 18-25.

DIRECTIONS: Questions 18 through 25 are to be answered SOLELY on the basis of the information given in the table below.

TABLE OF INFORMATION ABOUT GARDEN HOSE ON HAND

Commodity Index Number	Kind and Diameter of Hose (in inches)	Number of Feet Per Roll	Weight Per Roll lbs.	Weight Per Roll oz.	Cost Per Roll	Number of Rolls on Hand
SL 14171	Plastic, 3/4 in.	25	6	5	$ 5.90	20
SL 14172	Plastic, 3/4 in.	50	12	5	9.90	50
SL 14271	Plastic, 5/8 in.	25	4	7	4.40	40
SL 14272	Plastic, 5/8 in.	50	8	10	7.40	50
SL 14273	Plastic, 5/8 in.	75	13	0	10.40	50
SL 14274	Plastic, 5/8 in.	100	17	0	13.40	100
SL 24171	Rubber, Reinforced, 3/4"	25	9	3	8.90	20
SL 24172	Rubber, Reinforced 3/4"	50	18	0	14.90	10
SL 24271	Rubber, Reinforced, 5/8"	25	6	2	6.20	40
SL 24272	Rubber, Reinforced, 5/8"	50	12	2	10.90	40
SL 24273	Rubber, Reinforced, 5/8"	75	18	0	15.20	60
SL 24274	Rubber, Reinforced, 5/8"	100	24	0	19.90	100

18. The total weight of all of the 25 foot rolls of rubber, reinforced, 5/8 inch garden hose on hand is _____ lbs.   18.____

    A. 175   B. 240   C. 245   D. 485

19. Ah order for 10 rolls of SL 14271, 17 rolls of SL 14274, and 22 rolls of SL 24271 will MOST NEARLY weigh _____ lbs.   19.____

    A. 333   B. 423   C. 468   D. 472

20. The total cost of 12 rolls of 100 foot plastic, 5/8 inch garden hose is   20.____

    A. $124.80   B. $134.00   C. $160.80   D. $238.80

21. Assume that from the 40 rolls of SL 24272 and the 100 rolls of SL 24274, you ship one order of 10 rolls of SL 24272 and one order of 50 rolls of SL 24274.
    The total cost of all of the SL 24272 and the SL 24274 garden hose still on hand, after filling these orders, is   21.____

    A. $479   B. $1,104   C. $1,322   D. $1,451

22. Assume that 15% of all the 100 foot rolls of plastic garden hose and rubber reinforced garden hose are found defective.
    Then, the total cost of the defective hose is   22.____

    A. $199.00   B. $298.00   C. $333.00   D. $499.50

23. The stock on hand of which one of the following sizes and types of garden hose has the GREATEST total cost?
SL

    A. 14171   B. 14271   C. 24171   D. 24172

24. If 3/4 inch plastic garden hose is taken from the 50 foot rolls, then the cost of one foot of such hose is MOST NEARLY

    A. 20¢   B. 23¢   C. 26¢   D. 29¢

25. If it takes one worker one hour to inspect 20 rolls of garden hose for defects, the LEAST amount of time it will take two workers to inspect ALL the rolls of garden hose in stock is _____ hours _____ minutes.

    A. 14; 30   B. 15; 50   C. 24; 10   D. 29; 0

KEY (CORRECT ANSWERS)

1. D		11. C	
2. A		12. D	
3. B		13. B	
4. D		14. C	
5. A		15. B	
6. B		16. D	
7. D		17. C	
8. C		18. C	
9. A		19. C	
10. C		20. C	

21. C
22. D
23. C
24. A
25. A

EXAMINATION SECTION
TEST 1

DIRECTIONS: Each question or incomplete statement is followed by several suggested answers or completions. Select the one that BEST answers the question or completes the statement. *PRINT THE LETTER OF THE CORRECT ANSWER IN THE SPACE AT THE RIGHT.*

1. Of the following, the hazard MOST likely to damage rubber tubes in storage is   1.____

    A. breakage
    B. combustion
    C. corrosion
    D. deterioration

2. Of the following, the hazard MOST likely to damage vacuum tubes in storage is   2.____

    A. breakage
    B. corrosion
    C. deterioration
    D. evaporation

3. In checking large numbers of incoming supplies of a single item, the BEST practice to follow is to   3.____

    A. count the total number of containers received and only count the number of units in some of the containers
    B. count the total number of containers received only in those shipments where there is some doubt
    C. open all exterior containers received and count the number of containers inside when there are interior containers
    D. open all exterior and interior containers received and count the exact number of units

4. Some experts advise that barrels containing liquids should be turned occasionally. The BEST reason for this is to   4.____

    A. enable a check of the condition of the barrel
    B. enable a check of the condition of the contents
    C. keep the contents well mixed
    D. prevent the wood from drying out

5. For day-to-day protection when working in a room or enclosure containing combustible or explosive gases or gasolines, it would be MOST advisable to wear   5.____

    A. a general purpose gas mask
    B. a synthetic rubber suit
    C. non-sparking shoes
    D. rubber-framed goggles

6. The one of the following which is NOT recommended as a method of reducing the possibility of spontaneous combustion of burlap bags is to   6.____

    A. air them out before stacking
    B. dampen them slightly before stacking
    C. keep them off concrete floors
    D. keep them away from brick walls

7. When oxygen is leaking from a gas cylinder and the valve cannot close properly, the MOST advisable course of action to take while waiting for the valve to be repaired is to

   A. evacuate the building
   B. have it sent to a using agency before more oxygen is lost
   C. place the cylinder in the room with the poorest ventilation
   D. remove the cylinder from the building

8. Assume that you have to move four cartons to a location about 35 feet away. Each carton weighs 20 pounds and measures 2' x 8' x 4'.
   Of the following, the method of moving the cartons which would ordinarily be BEST is to

   A. have a team of two men make four trips
   B. have two teams of two men each carry two cartons
   C. make one trip using a four-wheel handtruck
   D. make one trip using a two-wheel handtruck

9. Assume that you have to move one carton to a location about 15 feet away. The carton weighs about 30 pounds and measures 8" x 18" x 24".
   Of the following, the method of moving the carton which would ordinarily be BEST is to

   A. have one man carry it
   B. have two men carry it
   C. put it on a two-wheel handtruck
   D. put it on a four-wheel handtruck

10. Assume that you have to move ten 45-pound cartons to a location about 75 feet away. Each carton measures 24" x 24" x 24".
    Of the following, the method of moving the cartons which would ordinarily be BEST is to

    A. load them on a pallet and use a forklift truck
    B. load them on a skid and push the skid
    C. load them on a trailer and pull it with a tractor
    D. use a portable conveyor

Questions 11-16.

DIRECTIONS: Questions 11 through 16 are to be answered SOLELY on the basis of the following table.

REPORT OF SEMI-ANNUAL INVENTORY

Article	Physical Inventory				Perpetual Inventory		Adjustment	
	Unit	Qty.	Price	Amt.	Qty.	Amt.	Qty.	Amt.
Batteries, flashlight	ea.	63	.08	5.04	60	14.80	+3	+.24
Bolts, flat head with square nuts, 100 in box	box	23	1.47	33.80	25	36.75		
Fuse, 15 amp, 4 in box	box	80	.07	5.60	80	5.60		
Fuse, 20 amp, 4 in box	box	77	.07	5.39	80	5.60	3	.21
Tape, friction, 50 ft. to a roll	roll	45	.22	9.90	45	9.90		
Washers, 100 in can 1/8" beveled	can	35	.32	11.20	35	11.20		
3/8" beveled	can	41	.33	13.53	45	14.85	4	1.32
Totals				84.47		88.70		

11. In the above report, for which item is there an INCORRECT entry?   11.____

    A. 15 amp. fuses   B. Friction tape
    C. Flashlight batteries   D. 1/8" washers

12. In the above report, adjustments were omitted for _____ article(s).   12.____

    A. one   B. two   C. three   D. four

13. After all appropriate entries have been made in the Adjustment column, the total which must be deducted from the book value of the inventory is   13.____

    A. $1.53   B. $1.77   C. $4.23   D. $4.71

14. The quantities shown in Perpetual Inventory exceed those shown in Physical Inventory by a total of   14.____

    A. 4   B. 6   C. 10   D. 12

15. The cost of ten washers, 1/8" beveled, is MOST NEARLY   15.____

    A. $.003   B. $.032   C. $.320   D. $3.20

16. The cost of 24 fuses is MOST NEARLY   16.____

    A. $.28   B. $.42   C. $.80   D. $1.68

17. Assume that you are in charge of a group of four men who are to carry an oak beam measuring 8" x 8" x 18' from one point to another.
Of the following, the BEST method of carrying the beam is to have

    A. the men arrange themselves at equal distances along one side of the beam and carry the beam at their sides
    B. the men arrange themselves at equal distances on opposite sides of the beam and carry the beam at waist height
    C. the men arrange themselves in order of height along the beam so that the beam may be carried on the shoulders of all of the men
    D. two men stand at one end of the beam and two men at the other end in order to lift the beam on to the shoulders of the two strongest men

18. Although the old model of a certain item has been replaced by a new model which is interchangeable with the old model, most requisitions call specifically for the old model. Since your stock of the old model is almost depleted, it would be MOST advisable for you to

    A. establish a carefully regulated system of priorities based on need
    B. inform the source of your supply of the continued demand for the old model
    C. inform the using agencies or individuals of the feasibility of substituting the new model
    D. substitute the new model whenever the old model is called for

19. An assistant stockman is assigned by you to take physical inventory of a particular small part stored in several open boxes. This part is of uniform size and is packaged 100 to a box. He returns in an unusually short time with the count. His explanation for his speed is that he consolidated all the items as much as possible so that all except one box were full. He multiplied 100 by the number of boxes and added the number of additional parts left.
Of the following, the MOST advisable course of action for you to take is to

    A. compliment him on his efficiency
    B. explain the proper way of taking inventory
    C. have him watch a more experienced worker take inventory
    D. suggest that he ask permission before changing procedure

20. In determining the number of months of supply to be ordered at one time, the LEAST important of the following factors is the

    A. average market price
    B. deterioration rate
    C. discount for quantity
    D. money available for purchasing

21. A check during physical inventory has revealed that many of the bottles of alcohol do not contain sixteen ounces as indicated on the labels.
Of the following, the MOST advisable action to take FIRST is to

    A. check future shipments by the vendor immediately upon their arrival
    B. see if the bottles are tightly capped
    C. see if the cartons are wet
    D. question your subordinates about the situation

22. Of the following, the FIRST thing which should be done in order to determine the reason for a discrepancy between the perpetual inventory card and the bin card or other similar record is to

    A. check the original requisitions
    B. compare each transaction listed on both cards
    C. ascertain whether any stock has been transferred to another warehouse
    D. question all personnel involved

23. Items such as tools are sometimes issued on a temporary basis and are to be returned after use so that they may be issued again when needed. In such cases, a record of each withdrawal

    A. need not be kept
    B. should be made on an inventory card
    C. should be made on a locator card
    D. should be made on a separate register

24. Assume that you have 100 boxes of a particular item on hand. Since this is the minimum order point, you have already ordered 300 boxes, which is the usual 6 months' supply. This order has not yet been delivered, and you have just received a requisition for 1,000 boxes.
    Of the following, the MOST advisable action for you to take FIRST is to

    A. order an additional 1,000 boxes
    B. order an additional 1,300 boxes
    C. ascertain the reason for such a requisition
    D. inform the ordering agency that the requisition cannot be filled immediately

Questions 25-27.

DIRECTIONS: Questions 25 through 27 are based on the following method of obtaining a reorder point: multiply the monthly rate of consumption by the lead time (in months) and add the minimum balance.

25. If the reorder point is 250 units, the lead time is 2 months, and the average monthly rate of consumption is 75 units, then the minimum balance is _____ units.

    A. 75   B. 100   C. 150   D. 250

26. If the lead time is 30 days, the minimum balance is 200 units, and the average monthly rate of consumption is 100 units, then the reorder point is _____ units.

    A. 100   B. 200   C. 300   D. 400

27. If the reorder point is 300 units, the lead time is 2 months, and the minimum balance is 100 units, then the average monthly rate of consumption is _____ units.

    A. 50   B. 100   C. 200   D. 300

28. You are planning to submit an initial order for a new item. You estimate that you will issue 100 per month, and you want to have a two-month supply in reserve. You will reorder this item every six months. Your initial order should be for

    A. 200   B. 600   C. 700   D. 800

29. For a particular item, the reorder point is established at 585. If the average rate of consumption is 130 and the lead time is 3 months, then the amount which should be on hand when the new delivery is received is

   A. 130   B. 195   C. 260   D. 325

30. You have room in the storehouse for 750 cartons of a certain item. Assume that you issue 125 cartons per month and keep a one-month supply in reserve. Delivery time is thirty days.
   Which of the following would it be MOST appropriate to order under these conditions?
   _____ every _____ months.

   A. 250; 3   B. 500; 3   C. 375; 4   D. 500; 4

31. Using maximum loads when transporting stock is

   A. *desirable* because it results in fewer trips
   B. *desirable* because it simplifies accounting and clerical work
   C. *undesirable* because it shortens the life of the equipment
   D. *undesirable* because it strains the capacity of the workers

32. Of the following, the BEST single basis for determining the desirability of purchasing new stock-handling equipment is the

   A. ability of the workers to handle the equipment
   B. condition of the present equipment
   C. estimated savings in costs
   D. size of the warehouse or stock facility

33. Frequent rest periods are MOST desirable when

   A. the men have been doing a good job
   B. the morale of the men is low
   C. there is a great deal of heavy work
   D. there is not too much work

34. In terms of plant economy, a storehouse is operating at GREATEST efficiency when it stores _____ stock that it is designed to hold.

   A. 10% less   B. 10% more
   C. 50% more   D. the exact amount of

35. Of the following, the one which a foreman or supervisor can MOST readily increase or improve is an employee's ability to

   A. get along with his fellow workers
   B. perform technical aspects of his job
   C. supervise others
   D. use good judgment in unusual situations

36. On one day, a certain piece of stock-handling equipment is not used at all. On the next day, several men are waiting to use it.
   This situation can BEST be corrected by

   A. having the men do the work manually
   B. keeping additional equipment available

C. posting a schedule for the use of the equipment
D. rearranging the work of the men

37. Despite all your efforts to streamline the work and make it more efficient, there still seems to be more work than you and your men can handle in a normal work week.
The MOST advisable course of action for you to take FIRST is to

   A. discuss the matter with your supervisor
   B. request more mechanical equipment
   C. request permission for overtime work
   D. tell your men that everyone will have to work a little harder

38. Assume that a subordinate tells you that he has made a mistake in filling out certain records.
The MOST advisable action for you to take FIRST is to

   A. explain how the job should have been done
   B. get another subordinate to do the job correctly
   C. tell him how to correct his mistake
   D. tell him to forget it but to do it correctly next time

39. Your supervisor gives you instructions which you feel are contrary to good storage procedure.
The MOST advisable action for you to take FIRST is to

   A. attempt to get additional support for your point of view
   B. follow his instructions without question
   C. suggest your method of doing the work
   D. say nothing but do the job the way you feel it should be done

40. You have reason to believe that one of your men is taking home merchandise from the storehouse. You question the man about this. He shows you that it was obsolete material of no value which was not salvageable and was about to be discarded.
Under these circumstances, the MOST appropriate action for you to take is to

   A. have him return the merchandise
   B. report the matter to your supervisor
   C. say nothing further
   D. tell the man that he should have asked your permission

41. Three new men have just been assigned to work under your supervision. Every time you give them an assignment, one of these men asks you several questions.
Of the following, the MOST advisable action for you to take is to

   A. assure him of your confidence in his ability to carry out the assignment correctly without asking so many questions
   B. have all three men listen to your answers to these questions
   C. point out that the other two men do the job without asking so many questions
   D. tell him to see if he can get the answers from other workers before coming to you

42. One of the men in your crew has continually been making derogatory statements about the personal life of one of the other men.
Of the following, it would probably be MOST advisable for you to

   A. attempt to obtain a transfer for the man who is the subject of the derogatory statements
   B. ignore the matter unless it has any effect on the work
   C. point out to your crew some of the weak spots in the character of the man who is making derogatory statements
   D. tell the man to stop making derogatory statements

43. Two of your subordinates suggest that you recommend a third man for an above-standard service rating because of his superior work.
You should

   A. ask the two subordinates whether the third man knows that they intended to discuss this matter with you
   B. explain to the two subordinates that an above-standard service rating for one man would have a detrimental effect on many of the other men
   C. recommend the man for an above-standard service rating if there is sufficient justification for it
   D. tell the two subordinates that the matter of service ratings is not their concern

44. At a meeting with your subordinates, which you have called in order to determine the best ways of dealing with some departmental policies, some of the men interrupt with comments and suggestions.
Of the following, the MOST advisable course of action for you to take in MOST cases is to

   A. encourage full but orderly participation by all the men
   B. end the meeting and issue a bulletin instead
   C. tell them to hold their comments and questions until after you have finished
   D. tell those who interrupt that they are being unfair to the others

45. When one of your subordinates takes unusually long lunch hours, you tell him that this practice must stop.
Of the following, the BEST reason for speaking to him about this is that

   A. he will take even longer lunch hours unless you speak to him
   B. morale of your other subordinates may be impaired unless the situation is corrected
   C. work cannot be done in time unless the practice is discontinued
   D. your other subordinates will take the same amount of time for lunch as he does

46. You have just been assigned a new employee who has had a college education but has had no experience in stock work. Of the following, the BEST course of action for you to take is to

   A. attempt to have him transferred as soon as possible
   B. explain to him that he probably would not like the work
   C. make special efforts to ease his relationships with the other workers
   D. treat him the same as you would treat any other new worker

47. The morale of your subordinates seems unusually high. They tell you that it is because they have heard that one of them is to get a provisional promotion. You know definitely that this is not true.
    The MOST advisable action for you to take is to

    A. act as if you are happy to hear the good news
    B. let the situation take its normal course
    C. report the matter to your supervisor
    D. tell them that, so far as you know, the rumor is not justified

48. In most cases, the FIRST step to take in the event of serious injury in the storeroom is to

    A. search the employee for instructions pertaining to medical care
    B. send for medical help
    C. take the employee to a hospital
    D. treat the injury

49. An employee has accidentally cut his arm and is bleeding profusely.
    The one of the following which should NOT be done is to

    A. apply pressure above the injury
    B. give the employee a mild stimulant
    C. keep the employee at complete rest
    D. raise the bleeding part

50. When gasoline and all other highly inflammable substances are stored outdoors, the *No Smoking* rule should be

    A. observed for indoor and outdoor storage areas
    B. observed for indoor storage areas only
    C. observed for outdoor storage areas only
    D. eliminated for indoor and outdoor storage areas

KEY (CORRECT ANSWERS)

1. D	11. C	21. B	31. A	41. B
2. A	12. A	22. B	32. C	42. D
3. A	13. C	23. D	33. C	43. C
4. D	14. B	24. C	34. D	44. A
5. C	15. B	25. B	35. B	45. B
6. B	16. B	26. C	36. D	46. D
7. D	17. A	27. B	37. A	47. D
8. C	18. C	28. D	38. C	48. B
9. A	19. A	29. B	39. C	49. B
10. A	20. A	30. D	40. D	50. A

EXAMINATION SECTION
TEST 1

DIRECTIONS: Each question or incomplete statement is followed by several suggested answers or completions. Select the one that BEST answers the question or completes the statement. *PRINT THE LETTER OF THE CORRECT ANSWER IN THE SPACE AT THE RIGHT.*

1. For the GREATEST economy in transporting stock, one should   1.____

    A. divide the load into as many easily managed units as possible
    B. replace machines with men whenever possible
    C. transport as large a load as possible at one time
    D. utilize conveyor belts for most transporting

2. Assume that a new piece of equipment has been devised that would cut the labor cost of a certain major operation 75% and the time 50%. The monetary savings to the city would be such that the machine would pay for itself in one year. However, the old equipment is still in good working condition.   2.____
The MOST advisable recommendation to make is that the

    A. *new* equipment be purchased
    B. *new* equipment be purchased only if the old equipment can be sold at a reasonable price
    C. *new* equipment be rented
    D. *old* equipment be retained until there is moderate deterioration

3. Economy in handling stock can be measured BEST in terms of the   3.____

    A. cost of the equipment used
    B. cost of stock-handling operations
    C. overhead cost plus depreciation of equipment
    D. salaries being paid to the men

4. It is MOST economical and efficient to have good lighting available in   4.____

    A. all parts of the storehouse
    B. packing areas only
    C. receiving areas only
    D. storage areas only

5. If a great deal of heavy work must be completed by men under your supervision, it is MOST advisable, when possible, to   5.____

    A. give frequent rest periods
    B. have the men work overtime
    C. have the men listen to lively music while working
    D. shorten the lunch hour

6. A storehouse USUALLY operates at GREATEST efficiency when it stores _____ stock than it is designed to hold.   6.____

    A. slightly less   B. slightly more
    C. substantially more   D. the exact amount of

7. Usually, a report should be prepared with AT LEAST

   A. one copy so that there is a copy for future reference
   B. two copies so that the report can be sent to more than one person
   C. two copies so that there is an extra copy for your supervisor
   D. three copies so that there will be sufficient copies if they are needed

8. Of the following, the one which can MOST easily be increased or improved in an employee by his foreman or supervisor is

   A. ability to learn   B. aptitude
   C. common sense   D. knowledge

9. Two men under your supervision who are required to work together are not able to get along with each other. You have attempted to remedy this situation but without any success. One is an older man who has been in the section for many years, and the other is a recently-appointed younger man. Both men are capable employees.
   Of the following, the MOST advisable course of action for you to take is to recommend that the

   A. older man be transferred
   B. two men be given below-average service ratings
   C. younger man be discharged at the end of his probationary period
   D. younger man be transferred

10. Inefficient scheduling of work should be suspected when one notes that there are several men

    A. absent from work   B. in the rest room
    C. loading a truck   D. waiting to use equipment

11. *It is better to haul than to carry.*
    The PRIMARY reason for this statement is that

    A. stock should not be placed on top of any movable equipment
    B. stockmen should not be allowed to carry stock for any great distance
    C. the same power can usually pull more than it can carry
    D. there is less danger of damage when stock is hauled

12. After you have given a newly-appointed subordinate complete instructions on how to use a handtruck, you should usually

    A. assign him to work with another subordinate
    B. go over the instructions once more
    C. let him use the handtruck while you watch him
    D. tell him about the importance of the work

13. One of your subordinates tells you that he wants to submit a suggestion to the suggestion program regarding the operation of the storeroom but that he wants your advice first. The MOST advisable course of action for you to take is to

    A. advise him that any suggestions concerning the storeroom should be made directly to you
    B. give him advice provided he includes your name on the suggestion

C. give him the advice he needs
D. tell him that it would not be fair if you were to give him any help

14. Assume that you are in charge of one section of a storehouse. When the man in charge of an adjoining section resigns, you are asked to assume that job in addition to your own. After several weeks, you find that it is impossible for you to provide adequate supervision for both sections.
Of the following, the BEST course of action for you to take is to

    A. ask your supervisor for a transfer
    B. assign one subordinate in each section the job of supervision
    C. divide your time between the two sections
    D. inform your supervisor of the facts

15. Your subordinates tell you that, in your absence, your supervisor gave them orders which differed from those which you had given them.
In this case, you should

    A. discuss the matter with your subordinates to determine which orders are correct
    B. discuss the matter with your supervisor
    C. tell your subordinates to follow your orders
    D. tell your subordinates to follow your supervisor's orders

16. Assume that one of your subordinates made an error in recording an issue of stock. The mistake was found and corrected, but your subordinate seems rather depressed about the matter.
Of the following, the MOST advisable course of action for you to take is to

    A. ignore the entire situation unless it happens again
    B. praise him
    C. reprimand him mildly
    D. show him how he can avoid such a mistake in the future

17. Assume that you have the following equipment available: two forklift trucks, one tractor, six trailers, and four handtrucks.
In order to move twenty pallet loads 200 yards in a storehouse, it would be MOST advisable for you to use the

    A. forklift trucks
    B. forklift trucks, the tractor, and the trailers
    C. handtrucks, the tractor, and the trailers
    D. tractor and the trailers

18. Small cartons to be stored for a period of a year would usually be BEST stored on

    A. dollies   B. pallets   C. the floor   D. trailers

19. The one of the following types of equipment which should generally be used to collect a small number of items from various parts of the storehouse for a single shipment is a

    A. four-wheel truck   B. pallet
    C. skid   D. two-wheel truck

20. In a large city storehouse, main aisles used for movement of materials should usually be NOT less than _____ ft.

    A. 1   B. 2   C. 4   D. 6

21. An aisle used only as a fire aisle should be APPROXIMATELY _____ feet wide.

    A. 2   B. 5   C. 8   D. 10

22. When a perishable commodity is received at the storeroom, the factor which is generally LEAST important to consider when deciding where to store it is the

    A. activity of the commodity
    B. size and weight of the commodity
    C. temperature and humidity of the storage areas
    D. total storage capacity of the storeroom

23. Ten cartons of a certain item are stacked on each of ten pallets standing in a row. Assume that the men and equipment mentioned below are available.
In order to move the cartons, with or without the pallets, from their place in the storehouse into a waiting truck, a distance of 25 yards, it would be MOST efficient to

    A. form a line of men to pass the cartons into the truck
    B. have a forklift truck take each pallet load separately and load it on the truck
    C. have one man move each pallet load with a hand lift pallet truck
    D. transfer the cartons from the pallets to a single tractor trailer train and then load them on the truck

24. The one of the following circumstances in which it would be MOST appropriate to use a fixed-platform power truck rather than a forklift truck is when

    A. loading a railroad car
    B. miscellaneous small items must be selected for a single shipment
    C. the load must be carried over a long distance
    D. there is a shortage of manpower

25. Storing small items in their original containers is a

    A. *bad* practice because it encourages laziness
    B. *bad* practice because it is disorderly
    C. *good* practice because it decreases handling
    D. *good* practice because it eliminates the need for shelves and bins

KEY (CORRECT ANSWERS)

1. C
2. A
3. B
4. A
5. A

6. D
7. A
8. D
9. D
10. D

11. C
12. C
13. C
14. D
15. B

16. D
17. B
18. B
19. A
20. D

21. A
22. D
23. B
24. B
25. C

———

TEST 2

DIRECTIONS: Each question or incomplete statement is followed by several suggested answers or completions. Select the one that BEST answers the question or completes the statement. *PRINT THE LETTER OF THE CORRECT ANSWER IN THE SPACE AT THE RIGHT.*

1. Assume that you have to move two cartons to a location about 50 feet away. Each carton weighs 10 pounds and measures 2' x 4' x 4'.
   Of the following, the method of moving the cartons which would ordinarily be BEST is to

   A. have two men carry each carton
   B. make one trip using a two-wheel handtruck
   C. make two trips using a two-wheel handtruck
   D. put both cartons on a four-wheel handtruck

2. Assume that you have to move two cartons to a location about 25 feet away. Each carton weighs 10 pounds and measures 6" x 12" x 18".
   Of the following, the method of moving the cartons which would ordinarily be BEST is to

   A. have one man carry both cartons in one trip
   B. have one man make two trips
   C. put both cartons on a four-wheel handtruck
   D. put both cartons on a two-wheel handtruck

3. Assume that you have to move twenty 10-pound cartons to a location about 100 feet away.
   Of the following, the method of moving the cartons which would ordinarily be BEST is to

   A. get a team of men to carry them by hand
   B. load them on a pallet and use a forklift truck
   C. load them on a skid and push the skid
   D. make a line of men and pass them from hand to hand

4. Assume that you have to move fifty pallets from one location in the warehouse to another about 250 feet away. Of the following, the equipment that you would need to do the job MOST efficiently is

   A. forklift truck, tractor, trailers
   B. four-wheel handtruck, portable elevator
   C. two-wheel handtruck, tractor, trailers
   D. two-wheel handtruck, trailers

5. The principle of *first-in, first-out* should generally be applied

   A. only to commodities subject to deterioration
   B. only to dated commodities
   C. only to perishable commodities
   D. to most commodities

6. A worker who is lifting a heavy object from the floor to a shoulder height position should preferably

   A. bend his knees, keep his back straight, and jerk the object to shoulder height in one quick motion
   B. bend his knees, keep his back straight, and lift to shoulder height in a slow continuous motion
   C. lift the object waist high, rest one end of it on a ledge, and then, while bending the knees, raise it to shoulder height
   D. lift the object waist high, rest one end of it on a ledge, and then, while keeping the knees straight, raise it to shoulder height

7. You have in stock a full drum of liquid which is lying on its side. You assign two men to stand it upright.
   The proper position for the men to take is for _____ to stand _____ of the drum.

   A. both; at the bottom end
   B. both; at the top end
   C. each; on opposite ends
   D. each; on opposite sides

8. Assume that you are employed in a well organized storehouse. Your stock records indicate that 450 units of a certain commodity are in stock. You count these items on a shelf and find only 175.
   The MOST advisable action for you to take FIRST is to

   A. consult the locator system
   B. count these items again
   C. recompute the stock balance
   D. report the shortage

9. A certain item is stored in a number of locations throughout a storeroom. You have counted the items in each location and added the numbers to get the total.
   Of the following, the BEST way to make sure that your figures are correct is to

   A. add the numbers again, using a different method
   B. add the numbers again, using the same method
   C. count the items again and recompute
   D. move all the items to one location

10. In taking inventory, you count much more of a certain iten than is shown on the inventory card.
    Of the following, the MOST advisable action for you to take FIRST is to

    A. put an adjusting entry on the inventory card
    B. refer the matter to your supervisor
    C. review all requisitions since the last inventory record
    D. recheck the figures on the card

11. Assume that paper is issued at the rate of 500 reams per month. Three-hole punches are issued at the rate of 1 a month.
    Of the following alternatives, it would probably be MOST practical and economic to order

    A. 500 reams per month and one three-hole punch per month
    B. 1,500 reams four times a year and 12 three-hole punches once a year
    C. 2,000 reams three times a year and 60 three-hole punches once every 5 years
    D. 18,000 reams once every 3 years and 36 three-hole punches once every 3 years

12. Assume that the price of an item is much lower during the months of June, July, and August However, you issue it throughout the year at the rate of 100 per month. The delivery time is one month, and you keep a one-month's reserve on hand at all times. You have enough room for 600 items.
    Of the following, it would ordinarily be BEST for you to order

    A. 200 in June, 500 in August, and 500 in January
    B. 400 in June, 400 in August, and 400 in December
    C. 600 in July and 600 in December
    D. 500 in June, 200 in July, and 500 in August

13. Assume that one of the items which you stock is issued only during April, May, and June at the rate of 400 per month. You keep a one-month's supply on hand at all times, although you have sufficient room for an unlimited supply. The delivery time is one month.
    Assuming that there are sufficient funds available at all times, it would probably be BEST for you to order

    A. 100 each month of the year
    B. 400 in March, 400 in April, and 400 in May
    C. 400 in April, 400 in May, and 400 in June
    D. 1,200 in March

14. Assume that you stock an item which deteriorates rapidly after 2 months. This item is issued at an average rate of 100 per month. The delivery time is one month. You keep a reserve supply of 20.
    If these figures are maintained, you should order _____ iteris once _____ month(s).

    A. 100; a   B. 200; every two
    C. 220; every two   D. 300; every three

15. Assume that you have 50 boxes of a particular item on hand. The minimum order point is 100, and you have already ordered 300 boxes, which is the usual 3-months' supply. This order has not yet been delivered, and you have just received a special requisition for an additional 300 boxes.
    Of the following, the MOST advisable action for you to take is to order

    A. 300 boxes immediately
    B. 300 boxes as soon as your outstanding order has been received
    C. 600 boxes immediately
    D. 600 boxes at the end of the present 3-month period

16. When a new model of a certain item is manufactured, you still have in stock a number of items of the old model. The old model is usable, but all the requisitions call for the new model.
    Asking the requesting agencies or individuals to accept the old model instead is

    A. *desirable* because the best items should be issued last
    B. *desirable* because you will not be left with obsolete stock
    C. *undesirable* because it is interfering with their prerogatives
    D. *undesirable* because they should not be penalized for your errors

17. You are planning to submit an initial order for a new item. You estimate that you will issue 10 per month, and you want to have a one month's supply in reserve. You will reorder this item every three months.
    Your initial order should be for

    A. 10   B. 20   C. 30   D. 40

18. You have room in the storehouse for 1,000 cartons of a certain item. Assume that you issue 100 boxes per month and always keep a one-month's supply in reserve. You order supplies every six months. Delivery time is thirty days.
    Of the following, the MOST appropriate amount to order under usual circumstances is

    A. 500   B. 600   C. 700   D. 1,000

19. The PRINCIPAL disadvantage of having an order-picker fill two or more orders at one time is that

    A. more equipment is needed
    B. the order-picker will resent the burden
    C. the work must be scheduled more precisely
    D. there is greater chance of error

20. Of the following, the MOST important reason for having a physical inventory as well as a perpetual inventory is that a physical inventory

    A. enables a physical inspection of the items to determine their condition
    B. familiarizes the men with the stock
    C. gives a count of the number of items actually on hand
    D. provides an opportunity to clean up the area

21. Of the following conditions, the one which is properly represented by an annual stock turnover of 2.0 is _____ original stock has been replaced _____.

    A. half of the; during the year
    B. the; once during the year
    C. the; twice during the year
    D. the; once every two months

22. Of the following kinds of items, the one for which frequent inspections are MOST necessary is the item which is

    A. dated   B. heavy   C. plastic   D. small

23. Of the following items, the one for which physical counts should be made MOST frequently is

    A. nails B. pipes C. valves D. wrenches

24. In order to avoid any interruption in normal storehouse operations during physical inventory, it would be necessary to

    A. close each section as it is inventoried
    B. close the storehouse during inventory
    C. inventory only on alternate days
    D. inventory after working hours or on weekends

25. It would be desirable to reduce stock levels to a one month period when the item is

    A. *expensive* and can be readily obtained
    B. *expensive* and difficult to obtain
    C. *inexpensive* and can be readily obtained
    D. *inexpensive* and difficult to obtain

KEY (CORRECT ANSWERS)

1. D		11. B	
2. A		12. B	
3. B		13. D	
4. A		14. A	
5. D		15. A	
6. C		16. B	
7. D		17. D	
8. A		18. B	
9. C		19. D	
10. D		20. C	

21. C
22. A
23. D
24. D
25. A

EXAMINATION SECTION
TEST 1

DIRECTIONS: Each question or incomplete statement is followed by several suggested answers or completions. Select the one that BEST answers the question or completes the statement. *PRINT THE LETTER OF THE CORRECT ANSWER IN THE SPACE AT THE RIGHT.*

1. One of the results of understocking is that

    A. more money is tied up in stock
    B. stock must be ordered more frequently
    C. there is greater likelihood of obsolescence
    D. there is uneven distribution of materials in storage

    1.____

2. Assume that your re-order point is obtained by multiplying the monthly rate of consumption by the lead time (in months) and adding the minimum balance. For a particular item, the re-order point is established at 200 units.
    If the lead time is 2 months and the minimum balance is 100, then the average monthly rate of consumption is

    A. 50 B. 100 C. 150 D. 200

    2.____

3. If a certain item has shown no activity for two years, the MOST advisable action to take FIRST is to

    A. attempt to dispose of the item through salvage
    B. contact the using agencies or individuals to determine whether they can use the item
    C. contact the vendor to determine whether the item can be traded in
    D. write it off on the inventory control card

    3.____

4. The MOST important information on an inventory control card is that which gives the _____ of the item.

    A. identity   B. location
    C. rate of consumption   D. vendor

    4.____

5. A space 5 1/4 feet wide and 2 1/3 feet long has an area measuring MOST NEARLY _____ square feet.

    A. 9 B. 10 C. 11 D. 12

    5.____

6. One man is able to load two 2 1/2-ton trucks in one hour. To load ten such trucks, it will take ten men _____ hour(s).

    A. 1/2 B. 1 C. 2 D. 2 1/2

    6.____

7. If the average height of the stacks in your section of the storehouse is 10 feet, the area which will be occupied by 56,000 cubic feet of supplies is MOST likely to be

    A. 70' x 80' B. 60' x 90' C. 50' x 60' D. 560' x 100'

    7.____

2 (#1)

8. The number of cartons, each measuring two cubic feet, which can fit into a space which is 100 square feet in area and is 8 feet high is MOST NEARLY

   A. 50   B. 200   C. 400   D. 800

   8._____

9. When the floor area measures 200 feet by 200 feet and the maximum weight it can hold is 4,000 tons, then the safe floor load is _____ pounds per square foot.

   A. 20   B. 160   C. 200   D. 400

   9._____

10. A carton 1' x 1' x 3' measures _____ cubic yards.

    A. 1/3   B. 1/9   C. 3   D. 9

    10._____

11. You have received six cartons, each containing sixty boxes of staples, priced at $36.00 per carton.
    The price per box is

    A. $.10   B. $.60   C. $3.60   D. $6.00

    11._____

12. The amount of space, in cubic feet, required to store 100 boxes each measuring 24" x 12" x 6" is MOST NEARLY

    A. 10   B. 100   C. 168   D. 1008

    12._____

13. Assume that it takes an average of two man-hours to stack 1 ton of certain supplies. In order to stack 30 tons, the number of men required to complete the job in ten hours is

    A. 6   B. 10   C. 15   D. 30

    13._____

14. An area measures 20 feet by 22 1/2 feet. The floor load is 100 pounds per square foot. The total weight that can be stored in this area is MOST NEARLY _____ pounds.

    A. 450   B. 9,000   C. 22,500   D. 45,000

    14._____

15. The price of a certain type of linoleum is $.20 per square foot.
    The total cost of four pieces of 9' x 12' linoleum is MOST NEARLY

    A. $21   B. $80   C. $86   D. $432

    15._____

16. The number of board feet in a piece of lumber measuring 2 inches thick by 2 feet wide by 12 feet long is

    A. 12   B. 16   C. 24   D. 48

    16._____

17. If 39 3/8 ounces of a certain commodity are on hand and two requisitions are filled, one for 9 1/2 and one for 9 5/6 ounces, the number of ounces remaining are

    A. 18 2/3   B. 19 1/3   C. 20 1/24   D. 20 3/4

    17._____

18. In order to fill 96 bottles containing 3 fluid ounces each, the number of pints which would be needed is

    A. 9   B. 18   C. 32   D. 36

    18._____

19. If a section of a storeroom measures 29 feet 4 inches by 18 feet 3 inches, the total area is MOST NEARLY _____ square feet.

    A. 523   B. 524   C. 535   D. 537

    19._____

20. A discount of 1% is given on all purchases of over 100 brushes. An additional discount of 1% is given on all purchases of over 500 brushes.
    If 600 brushes are purchased at a list price of $2.07 each, the total cost is MOST NEARLY

    A. $1217   B. $1228   C. $1230   D. $2484

21. The following items are purchased: 30 locksets at $15.00 per dozen, and 10 gross of stove bolts at 1 1/2 cents each bolt.
    The total cost is MOST NEARLY

    A. $60   B. $180   C. $255   D. $470

22. The cost of one dozen pieces of screening, each measuring 4'6" by 5', at $.10 per square foot, is

    A. $22.50   B. $25.00   C. $27.00   D. $27.60

23. The amount of turpentine on hand is 39 gallons. One requisition is filled for 3 1/2 gallons, three additional requisitions are filled for 3 quarts each, and six requisitions are filled for 1 pint each.
    The quantity of turpentine remaining after all these requisitions have been filled is

    A. 32 gal.   B. 32 gal. 1 qt.
    C. 32 gal. 2 qts. D. 32 gal. 3 qts.

24. A shelf is 30" wide and 20" deep. The shelf is filled solid with 500 boxes, each measuring 2" x 3" x 5". The distance from the shelf to the top of the stacked boxes is

    A. 10"   B. 25"   C. 50"   D. 60"

25. In order to check on a shipment of 1000 articles, a sampling of 100 articles was carefully inspected.
    Of the sample, one article was wholly defective and 4 more were partly defective.
    On this basis, the percentage of completely acceptable articles in the original shipment is probably MOST NEARLY

    A. 5%   B. 10%   C. 95%   D. 100%

26. The one of the following which is NOT the name of a type of screwdriver is

    A. cabinet   B. flat-nose
    C. knife handle   D. spiral ratchet

27. Pupil Dental Record forms are likely to be used in GREATEST quantities by the

    A. Board of Education   B. Department of Health
    C. Department of Hospitals D. Department of Social Service

28. Crepe paper is likely to be requisitioned MOST frequently by the

    A. Board of Education   B. Department of Public Events
    C. Housing Authority   D. Transit Authority

29. Scalpels are likely to be requisitioned MOST frequently by the Department of   29._____

   A. Correction   B. Health
   C. Hospitals   D. Parks

30. Pruners are likely to be requisitioned MOST frequently by the   30._____

   A. Department of Parks   B. Department of Sanitation
   C. Reference Library   D. Transit Authority

31. Fustats are likely to be requisitioned MOST frequently by the   31._____

   A. Department of Markets   B. Fire Department
   C. Housing Authority   D. Police Department

32. Machine screws are usually purchased in large quantities by the   32._____

   A. bushel   B. gross   C. pound   D. score

33. A No. 10 can of fruit juice contains about   33._____

   A. eight ounces   B. one pint
   C. one quart   D. three quarts

34. Sulphuric acid is USUALLY purchased in large quantities by the   34._____

   A. carboy   B. drum   C. gallon   D. cylinder

35. The one of the following which is NOT a standard size of index card is   35._____

   A. 3x5   B. 4x6   C. 5 x 7   D. 5 x 8

36. The label on a package of mimeograph paper reads: Size 8 1/2 x 11, Basis 20. *Basis 20*   36._____
    refers to the

   A. color code for this type of paper
   B. quality and finish of the paper
   C. way in which the paper is packaged
   D. weight of the paper

37. You tell a man to separate and store cans of paint in a certain way. The man then asks   37._____
    you, *Why do you want me to do it this way?*
    You should answer his question by

   A. advising him to figure out the reason himself
   B. explaining to him why you want it done in that particular way
   C. repeating your instructions more slowly
   D. telling him to follow your instructions without asking any questions

38. Assume that an employee shows you that you have made an error in issuing certain   38._____
    instructions. You admit your error.
    Such action on your part is desirable PRIMARILY because

   A. the job may be done correctly
   B. your men will be encouraged to make similar corrections in the future
   C. you will gain a reputation for fairness
   D. your men will realize that you will not make errors of this type in the future

39. Assume that you have just been promoted. Your supervisor gives you detailed oral instructions as to how a particular category of stock should be stored. At the conclusion of his instructions, you realize that you do not fully understand how your supervisor wishes to have the stock stored.
Under these circumstances, you should

   A. ask an experienced worker to clarify your supervisor's instructions
   B. ask your supervisor to clarify anything that you do not understand
   C. ask your supervisor to put his instructions in writing
   D. carry out your supervisor's instructions as best as you can

40. You have reason to believe that one of your men is taking merchandise which does not belong to him from the storehouse. You question the man about this. He tells you that he borrowed the merchandise and intends to return it. Under these Circumstances, you should probably

   A. disregard the matter until such time as you have evidence which will stand up in court
   B. offer to accompany the man to his home to pick up the property in question
   C. report the matter to your supervisor
   D. tell the man to return the property as soon as he has finished using it

41. A truck which must be unloaded immediately arrives at the storehouse. You issue instructions to your crew as to how this should be done. One of your men strongly objects and says that your instructions are wrong. You listen to his reasons but you still think that you are right. Under these circumstances, you should

   A. ask for opinions from the other men in the crew as to how the job should be done
   B. contact another worker to get his opinion
   C. refer the matter to your supervisor for his decision
   D. tell the men to unload the truck in accordance with your instructions

42. Whenever you give an assignment to one of your experienced men, he asks you a great many questions about it although he has successfully performed similar assignments in the past. The time you spend in answering his many questions about minor details takes you away from more important work.
Under these circumstances, you should probably FIRST

   A. answer his questions in such a way that he will be discouraged from asking further questions
   B. ask the man to ask his questions of one of his fellow employees
   C. assure the man of your confidence in his ability to carry out the assignment
   D. tell the man that if the assignment is too difficult you will give it to someone who does not raise so many questions

43. You have reason to believe that one of the men in your crew gossips about you behind your back.
Under these circumstances, it is usually BEST to

   A. attempt to find out which of your men believes the gossip
   B. find out what the man's weak points are and bring them to the attention of your crew

C. ignore the matter
D. speak to the man about it and tell him to stop

44. Your supervisor gives you an assignment which you believe you cannot do since you do not have a sufficient number of men. You explain this to your supervisor but he tells you to get the job done.
You should

    A. do the best you can and keep your supervisor informed of the progress you are making
    B. report the matter to your main office
    C. insist that your supervisor give you his instructions in writing
    D. wait until your supervisor gives you more men before taking any action to carry out the assignment

45. Your crew consistently performs more work than the crew headed by another worker. The other worker tells you that the high performance of your crew makes his crew *look bad*.
Under these circumstances, it would be BEST for you to

    A. ignore the matter and have your crew continue working as before
    B. report the matter to your supervisor for disciplinary action
    C. slow your crew down somewhat to show the other man that you are willing to cooperate with him
    D. slow your crew down to the level of the other crew

46. Two of your men frequently argue with each other so that the work of your crew is disrupted.
You should FIRST

    A. attempt to find out why the men argue with each other
    B. speak to the two men privately regarding their possible transfer to another crew
    C. submit a report to your supervisor setting forth the facts
    D. tell both men that unless they stop arguing you will see that they are given below-standard service ratings

47. One of your men asks you to put him in for an above-standard service rating. His work has been good but it has not been above-standard.
You should tell the man that

    A. he has done good work but that in your judgment his work has not been above-standard
    B. if you recommend him for an above-standard service rating, you will have to do the same thing for most of the others in your crew
    C. you cannot discuss the matter with him but that you will discuss it with your supervisor
    D. you will speak to the other men in the crew and if no one objects you will recommend him for a higher service rating

48. You receive a memorandum from your supervisor in which he instructs you to make a large number of changes in the procedures for storing materials.
The BEST way to bring these changes to the attention of your crew is to

   A. post the memorandum on the bulletin board where everyone can read it
   B. meet individually with each member of your staff to discuss the changes
   C. hold a meeting with your crew and explain the changes to them
   D. see to it that the memorandum is circulated to and initialled by each member of the crew

49. Although you have frequently spoken to one of your men regarding the proper way of lifting heavy objects, he persists in ignoring your instructions. He says that he knows the proper way of lifting, that you do not, and that he does not intend to hurt himself by following your instructions.
Of the following, the BEST course of action for you to take is to

   A. assign the man to tasks which do not involve heavy lifting
   B. ignore the matter as long as the man does not hurt himself
   C. put your instructions on how to lift in writing and give a copy of your instructions to each man in the crew
   D. report the matter to your supervisor

50. You assign a man to take inventory of a certain item. The man gives you a figure which seems too high. Of the following, the BEST course of action for you to take is to

   A. accept the figure given to you by the man if he is willing to initial it
   B. accompany the man while he takes inventory again
   C. ask the man to take inventory again and tell him why
   D. take inventory yourself

KEY (CORRECT ANSWERS)

1. B	11. B	21. A	31. C	41. D
2. A	12. B	22. C	32. B	42. C
3. B	13. A	23. C	33. D	43. C
4. A	14. D	24. B	34. A	44. A
5. D	15. C	25. C	35. C	45. A
6. A	16. D	26. B	36. D	46. A
7. A	17. C	27. A	37. B	47. A
8. C	18. B	28. A	38. A	48. C
9. C	19. C	29. C	39. B	49. D
10. B	20. A	30. A	40. C	50. C

EXAMINATION SECTION
TEST 1

DIRECTIONS: Each question or incomplete statement is followed by several suggested answers or completions. Select the one that BEST answers the question or completes the statement. *PRINT THE LETTER OF THE CORRECT ANSWER IN THE SPACE AT THE RIGHT.*

1. Of the following, the MOST efficient way to handle and store heavy objects loaded on pallets in a warehouse is with the aid of a

    A. conveyor belt
    B. hand truck
    C. dolly
    D. forklift

    1._____

2. You receive 20 large glass containers of highly dangerous acid.
   Of the following, it would be SAFEST to store these glass containers in _____ area.

    A. a special designated
    B. a busy workshop
    C. the main storage
    D. the shipping and receiving

    2._____

Questions 3-7.

DIRECTIONS: Questions 3 through 7 each contains a description of a stock item which is incomplete. You are to answer each question by selecting the term which BEST completes the description of the item.

> EXAMPLE: Brush, tooth, adult size
> A. nylon bristle
> B. glass handle
> C. 18 inches
> D. fluoride

> The CORRECT answer is A, which completes the description of a toothbrush.

3. Polish, furniture, one quart can

    A. gasoline
    B. acid
    C. lemon oil
    D. glue substance

    3._____

4. Card, index, ruled, white

    A. bond   B. 3" x 5"   C. round   D. plastic

    4._____

5. Sugar, 1/6 ounce, individual package

    A. soft   B. mixed   C. sprinkled   D. granulated

    5._____

6. Pad, gauze, 2 in. x 2 in.

    A. sterile   B. paper   C. rubber   D. cold

    6._____

7. Shovel, snow, square point

    A. sweeper   B. duster   C. long handle   D. saw tooth

    7._____

8. There are times when birds find their way into a warehouse and make nests. This may cause problems to the store-keeping operations.
   Of the following, the MOST practical way to deal with this matter is to _____ the warehouse.

   A. place bird feed outside
   B. plant trees around
   C. provide bird perches in
   D. destroy bird nests in

9. Entries of incoming and outgoing stock items are made on individual stock cards for all the following reasons EXCEPT

   A. detecting possible stealing of the stock items
   B. keeping an accurate record of the stock items
   C. officially recording the entries of incoming and outgoing stock items
   D. showing your supervisor what a good job you can do

10. A particular stock item presently shows an inventory balance smaller than the inventory balance of the previous month.
    Of the following, this information shows you that the quantity of this particular item

    A. issued was more than the amount received
    B. issued was less than the amount received
    C. received was equal to the amount issued
    D. received was more than the amount issued

Questions 11-12.

DIRECTIONS: Questions 11 and 12 are to be answered on the basis of the information given in the following passage relating to an Executive Order by the Mayor.

The Commissioner of Investigation shall have general responsibility for the investigation and elimination of corrupt or other criminal activity, conflicts of interest, unethical conduct, misconduct, and incompetence by city agencies, by city officers and employees, and by persons regulated by, doing business with, or receiving funds directly or indirectly from the city, with respect to their dealings with the city. All agency heads shall be responsible for establishing, subject to review for completeness and inter-agency consistency by the Commissioner of Investigation, written standards of conduct for the officials and employees of their respective agencies, and fair and efficient disciplinary systems to maintain those standards of conduct. All agencies shall have an Inspector General who shall report directly to the respective agency head and to the Commissioner of Investigation and be responsible for maintaining standards of conduct as may be established in such agency under this Order. Inspectors General shall be responsible for the investigation and elimination of corrupt or other criminal activity, conflicts of interest, unethical conduct, misconduct and incompetence within their respective agencies. Except to the extent otherwise provided by law, the employment or continued employment of all existing and prospective Inspectors General and members of their staffs shall be subject to complete background investigations and approval by the Department of Investigation.

3 (#1)

11. According to the above passage, establishing written standards of conduct for each agency is the responsibility of the   11.____

   A. agency head
   B. Commissioner of Investigation
   C. Department of Investigation
   D. Inspector General

12. According to the above passage, maintaining standards of conduct within each agency is the responsibility of the   12.____

   A. agency head
   B. Commissioner of Investigation
   C. Department of Investigation
   D. Inspector General

Questions 13-16.

DIRECTIONS: Questions 13 through 16 are to be answered on the basis of the following information.

Assume that Warehouse X uses the following procedures for receiving stock. When a delivery is received, the stock handler who receives the delivery should immediately unpack and check the delivery. This check is to ensure that the quantity and kinds of stock items delivered match those on the purchase order which had been sent to the vendor. After the delivery is checked, a receiving report is prepared by the same stock handler. This receiving report should include the name of the shipper, the purchase order number, the description of the item, and the actual count or weight of the item. The receiving report, along with the packing slip, should then be checked by the stores clerk against the purchase order to make sure that the quantity received is correct. This is necessary before credit can be obtained from the vendor for any items that are missing or damaged. After the checking is completed, the stock items can be moved to the stockroom.

13. According to the procedures described above, the stock person who receives the delivery should   13.____

   A. placed the unopened delivery in a secure area for checking at a later date
   B. notify the stores clerk that the delivery has arrived and is ready for checking
   C. unpack the delivery and check the quantity and types of stock items against the purchase order
   D. closely examine the outside of the delivery containers for dents and damages

14. According to the procedures described above, credit can be obtained from the vendor   14.____

   A. *before* the stock handler checks the delivery of stock items
   B. *after* the stock handler checks the delivery of stock items
   C. *before* the stores clerk checks the receiving report against the purchase order
   D. *after* the stores clerk checks the receiving report against the purchase order

15. According to the procedures described above, all of the following information should be included when filling out a receiving report EXCEPT the

   A. purchase order number
   B. name of the shipper
   C. count or weight of the item
   D. unit cost per item

16. According to the procedures described above, after the stores clerk has checked the receiving report against the purchase order, the NEXT step is to

   A. move the stock items to the stockroom
   B. return the stock items received to the vendor
   C. give the stock items to the stock handler for final checking
   D. file the packing slip for inventory purposes

17. All of the following would be good ways for you to show an employee how to pack a box EXCEPT

   A. making sure that the employee can clearly see what you are doing
   B. going through the process slowly and carefully with the employee
   C. talking and working as quickly as you can, so that you don't bore the employee
   D. explaining the purpose of each step to the employee

18. You are starting to prepare a requisition for certain supplies, which must be done as soon as possible. A co-worker comes to you and asks you for your help in finding several stock items. You are told that finding these items will take some time. You decide to finish preparing the requisition first before you help your co-worker.
   Of the following, your action can BEST be described as

   A. *acceptable* because you must prepare the requisition as quickly as possible
   B. *unacceptable* because you should help your co-worker
   C. *acceptable* because your co-worker should be able to do the job alone
   D. *unacceptable* because you can finish preparing the requisition some other time

19. A newly-hired employee has just been assigned to work under your supervision. You want to be sure that the employee will do the job well and perform it properly. Of the following, the FIRST action you should take is to

   A. tell the employee exactly what has to be done and what is expected
   B. allow the employee to begin work on a difficult task immediately
   C. assign the employee to work with others who have little experience
   D. give the employee enough work to keep busy

20. You observe two of your subordinates, Mr. White and Mr. Wilson, lifting heavy items together. You see that Mr. White is not lifting the items properly while Mr. Wilson is.
   As the supervisor, the MOST appropriate action for you to take in this situation is to

   A. allow Mr. White time to learn by himself the correct way to lift heavy items
   B. have Mr. Wilson lift the heavy items by himself
   C. show Mr. White how to lift the heavy items properly
   D. advise Mr. Wilson to be very careful when working with Mr. White

21. One of your subordinates asks you to meet with him privately to discuss a personal problem which he feels is affecting his work performance. You know that you have a very busy work schedule every day.
    As the supervisor, the BEST way for you to handle this situation is to

    A. tell the subordinate that you are too busy to meet with him today but to try again in a few days
    B. tell the subordinate that it is not proper to discuss personal problems
    C. schedule a meeting with the subordinate for that same day
    D. tell the subordinate that you will hold a group meeting soon to discuss any problems

22. One of your responsibilities as a supervisor is to make sure that the unit area is cleaned up each day. You know that no one in your unit likes to do the cleaning. In order to minimize any dissatisfaction on the part of your subordinates, it would be BEST for you to assign this work

    A. to the strongest worker in your unit
    B. on a rotating basis
    C. to the slowest worker in your unit
    D. on a disciplinary basis

23. Two of your subordinates approach you and ask you to help them with a disagreement they are having about their job duties.
    The BEST approach for you to take in dealing with this situation is to

    A. tell the subordinates they should be able to settle the disagreement themselves
    B. check with other subordinates to find out if they can be of any help
    C. tell the subordinates to return to work and not to discuss the matter any further
    D. listen to what each subordinate has to say and then try to help them to reach an agreement

24. Assume that food items, as they are received, are clearly dated on the outside of each package by the receiver.
    If you assign one of your subordinates to pick the oldest stock of food items first when filling an order, then you should expect the subordinate to find the oldest stock by

    A. checking the date on the outside of each package
    B. opening each package and checking the items inside
    C. getting the information from the receiver
    D. asking you for the information

25. One of your subordinates has been arriving at work about one-half hour late every day for the past two weeks. However, the subordinate is able to complete the work on time and continues to do a good job.
    As the supervisor, the BEST way for you to deal with this matter is to

    A. talk to the subordinate in private about the lateness
    B. praise the subordinate for the good work being done
    C. say nothing because the subordinate is still doing the job well
    D. ask your superior what you should do

6 (#1)

26. Assume that you have outlined four steps you are going to take in solving a storekeeping problem. These steps are as follows:
    I. Analyze the facts.
    II. Define the problem.
    III. List possible solutions.
    IV. Get the facts.
Which one of the following shows the order of taking these steps that would be MOST effective in solving a problem?

   A. IV, II, I, III
   B. II, IV, I, III
   C. III, I, II, IV
   D. I, III, II, IV

26.____

Questions 27-31.

DIRECTIONS: Questions 27 through 31 are to be answered on the basis of the information given in Tables 1 and 2 of the DAILY PRODUCTIVITY REPORT shown below.

DAILY PRODUCTIVITY REPORT

Table 1

Standards Number of pieces packed per day	Unsatisfactory	Conditional	Satisfactory	Superior	Outstanding
	245 and below	246 to 289	290 to 347	348 to 405	406 and above

Table 2

Initials of the Packer	A.S	S.B.	B.D	L.M.	J.C	R.N.	B.G	C.A	D.F	E.R
Number of Pieces Packed Per Day	252	335	276	342	409	290	235	309	246	425

27. The number of packers whose productivity is *Outstanding* is

   A. 4   B. 3   C. 2   D. 1

27.____

28. The number of packers who come under the *Conditional* productivity standard is

   A. 1   B. 2   C. 3   D. 4

28.____

29. The percentage of packers whose productivity can be rated *Satisfactory* or higher is

   A. 30%   B. 40%   C. 50%   D. 60%

29.____

30. If every packer's daily productivity increased by 20 pieces, the number of packers whose productivity ratings would change to the NEXT standard is

   A. 4   B. 5   C. 6   D. 7

30.____

31. Which one of the following is an accurate statement that can be made based on the information shown in Tables 1 and 2? 31.____

    A. There are more packers whose productivity is above the maximum *Satisfactory* level than below the minimum *Satisfactory* level.
    B. There are more packers whose productivity is in the *Satisfactory* standard than in any one of the other four standards.
    C. The number of packers whose productivity is *Unsatisfactory* is equal to the number of packers whose productivity is *Outstanding*.
    D. There is at least one packer whose productivity is in each of the five standards.

Questions 32-35.

DIRECTIONS: Questions 32 through 35 are to be answered on the basis of the information given in the inventory tables shown below. Table 1 shows the amount of each item in stock according to the information contained on the perpetual inventory card for that item. Table 2 shows the amount of the same item in stock according to an inventory just completed by the staff.

Table 1

Perpetual Inventory Card	
Item No.	Amount of Stock
A107	2,564
A257	10,365
A342	7,018
A475	52,475
B026	16,207
B422	4,520
B717	21,431
B802	308
C328	594
C329	164
C438	723
C527	844

Table 2

Inventory Just Completed By Staff	
Item No.	Amount of Stock
A107	2,545
A257	10,356
A342	7,018
A475	52,475
B026	16,207
B422	4,505
B717	21,413
B802	308
C328	594
C329	143
C438	723
C527	854

32. In which one of the following items is there a difference between the amount of stock shown on the perpetual inventory card and in the inventory just completed? 32.____
    Item No.

    A. A257   B. B026   C. C328   D. C438

33. In which one of the following items is the difference GREATEST between the amount of stock shown on the perpetual inventory card and in the inventory just completed? 33.____
    Item No.

    A. A107   B. B422   C. B717   D. C329

34. The amount of stock shown for Item No. C527 on the inventory taken by the staff is greater than the amount shown on the perpetual inventory card.
Of the following, the LEAST likely reason for this difference is that the

   A. perpetual inventory card was not brought up to date
   B. staff did not take an accurate inventory
   C. information entered on the perpetual inventory card was inaccurate
   D. staff made an inventory on the wrong item

35. Which one of the following is an ACCURATE statement that can be made based on the information shown in Tables 1 and 2?

   A. More than half of the items listed show a difference between the amount of stock shown on the perpetual inventory card and in the inventory just completed.
   B. One-third of the items listed show the amount of stock on the perpetual inventory card and in the inventory just completed to be 10,000 or more.
   C. Less than half of the items listed show a difference between the amount of stock shown on the perpetual inventory card and in the inventory just completed.
   D. One-third of the items listed show the amount of stock on the perpetual inventory card and in the inventory just completed to be 10,000 or less.

36. You are preparing to hold a training session for your unit on the safe use of storekeeping equipment.
Of the following, the MOST important reason for you to give this training is to

   A. answer any questions your workers may have about the use of the equipment
   B. speed up the work done by the unit
   C. reduce the amount of time lost for equipment repair
   D. prevent accidents from happening when the equipment is being used

37. Of the following, the use of an *A* frame storage rack is MOST appropriate for storing

   A. pipes or tubular items
   B. crated goods
   C. office supplies and equipment
   D. empty pallets

38. Your warehouse is infested by rats. You have asked one of your subordinates to place rat traps throughout the warehouse in order to take care of the problem.
Of the following, the BEST way to use traps effectively is to

   A. keep the same bait in the traps at all times
   B. change the location of the traps frequently
   C. disinfect the unused traps daily
   D. place the traps in the busiest work areas

39. Of the following, the BEST way to determine how much of a certain item should be ordered each month is to

   A. call the vendor of a similar item to find out how often that item is delivered to your agency
   B. call another agency to find out how often deliveries of that item are made to that agency

C. keep an ongoing record of how much of the item is used during each month
D. increase the usual order so that your agency will never run out of that item

40. According to the information on a computer run, your stock of distilled water is short by 20 gallons. Of the following, the FIRST appropriate action you should take is to   40.____

   A. check your own records of all the deliveries and issuances
   B. let the computer unit know of their mistake
   C. balance the shortage by showing an issuance of 20 gallons in the next report
   D. buy 20 gallons of distilled water to make up the shortage

KEY (CORRECT ANSWERS)

1. D	11. A	21. C	31. B
2. A	12. D	22. B	32. A
3. C	13. C	23. D	33. D
4. B	14. D	24. A	34. D
5. D	15. D	25. A	35. B
6. A	16. A	26. B	36. D
7. C	17. C	27. C	37. A
8. D	18. A	28. C	38. B
9. D	19. A	29. D	39. C
10. A	20. C	30. A	40. A

TEST 2

DIRECTIONS: Each question or incomplete statement is followed by several suggested answers or completions. Select the one that BEST answers the question or completes the statement. *PRINT THE LETTER OF THE CORRECT ANSWER IN THE SPACE AT THE RIGHT.*

Questions 1-3.

DIRECTIONS: Questions 1 through 3 are to be answered on the basis of the information given in the passage below.

A filing system for requisition forms used in a warehouse will be of maximum benefit only if it provides ready access to information needed and is not too complex. How effective the system will be depends largely on how well the filing system is organized. A well-organized system usually results in a smooth-running operation.

When setting up a system for filing requisition forms, one effective method would be to first make an alphabetical listing of all the authorized requisitioning agencies. Then file folders should be prepared for each of these agencies and arranged alphabetically in file cabinets. Following this, each agency should be assigned a series of numbers corresponding to those on the blank requisition forms with which they will be supplied. When an agency then submits a requisition and it is filled, the form should be filed in numerical order in the designated agency folder. By using this system, any individual requisition form which is missing from its folder can be easily detected. Regardless of the filing system used, simplicity is essential if the filing system is to be successful.

1. According to the above passage, a filing system is MOST likely to be successful if it is   1._____

    A. alphabetical
    B. uncomplicated
    C. numerical
    D. reliable

2. According to the above passage, the reason numbers are assigned to each agency is to   2._____

    A. simplify stock issuing procedures
    B. keep a count of all incoming requisition forms
    C. be able to know when a form is missing from its folder
    D. eliminate the need for an alphabetical filing system

3. According to the above passage, which one of the following is an ACCURATE statement regarding the establishment of a well-organized filing system?   3._____

    A. Requisitioned stock items will be issued at a faster rate.
    B. Stock items will be stored in storage areas alphabetically arranged.
    C. Information concerning ordered stock items will be easily obtainable.
    D. Maximum productivity can be expected from each employee.

Questions 4-6.

DIRECTIONS: Questions 4 through 6 are to be answered on the basis of the information given in the chart below.

ITEM NUMBER TOTALS AS OF JANUARY 31

Item Number	Monthly Usage	Current Inventory	Time Required Between Ordering & Delivery of Item
1	460	1,000	1 month
2	475	1,500	2 months
3	225	1,500	4 months
4	500	2,500	5 months
5	1,150	1,950	2 months
6	775	4,700	5 months
7	850	1,700	2 months
8	900	3,600	3 months
9	175	525	2 months
10	1,325	5,300	3 months
11	225	900	4 months
12	425	1,500	1 month

4. Which one of the following, if not ordered by February 1, would cause the monthly usage to exceed the current inventory before new merchandise could be received?
Item Number

   A. 1   B. 4   C. 6   D. 10

4.____

5. Which one of the following must be ordered immediately because the current inventory cannot cover the monthly usage?
Item Number

   A. 2   B. 3   C. 5   D. 12

5.____

6. The date by which Item Numbers 8, 9, and 10 must be ordered so that the monthly usage does NOT exceed the current inventory is _____ .

   A. February 1   B. March 1
   C. April 1   D. May 1

6.____

7. When reviewing the monthly management report given to you by the supervisors of the units for which you are responsible, you find that one of the units has a large backlog of unfilled requisitions.
Of the following, the FIRST appropriate action you should take in handling this matter is to

   A. order more stock of all the items stored in your warehouse
   B. check with the supervisors of the other units and see how they would handle the matter
   C. immediately hire more workers to take care of the backlog
   D. consult with the supervisor of the unit which has the backlog to try to find the reason for it

7.____

8. You are assigning one of your subordinates, Mr. Jones, to do a task that he has never done before. It is important that he learn how to perform this task as soon as possible, but you do not have the time to train him. You decide to have a highly qualified subordinate, Mr. Smith, show him what must be done.
Of the following, your action concerning this situation can BEST be described as

   A. *acceptable* because it is appropriate for a supervisor to delegate work to a capable subordinate
   B. *unacceptable* because the training must be done by you, the supervisor
   C. *acceptable* because Mr. Smith can do a better job of training Mr. Jones than you can
   D. *unacceptable* because Mr. Smith will not be able to finish his regular duties

9. Jim Johnson has been on your staff for over four years. He has always been a conscientious and productive worker. About a month ago, his wife died; and since that time, his work performance has been very poor.
As his supervisor, which one of the following is the BEST way for you to deal with this situation?

   A. Allow Jim as much time as he needs to overcome his grief and hope that his work performance improves.
   B. Meet with Jim to discuss ways to improve his performance.
   C. Tell Jim directly that you are more concerned with his work performance than with his personal problem.
   D. Prepare disciplinary action on Jim as soon as possible.

10. You are responsible for the overall operation of a storehouse which is divided into two sections. Each section has its own supervisor. You have decided to make several complex changes in the storekeeping procedures which will affect both sections.
Of the following, the BEST way to make sure that these changes are understood by the two supervisors is for you to

    A. meet with both supervisors to discuss the changes
    B. issue a memorandum to each supervisor explaining the changes
    C. post the changes where the supervisors are sure to see them
    D. instruct one supervisor to explain the changes to the other supervisor

11. You have called a meeting of all your subordinates to tell them what has to be done on a new project in which they will all be involved. Several times during the meeting, you ask if there are any questions about what you have told them.
Of the following, to ask the subordinates whether there are any questions during the meeting can BEST be described as

    A. *inadvisable* because it interferes with their learning about the new project
    B. *advisable* because you will find out what they don't understand and have a chance to clear up any problems they may have
    C. *inadvisable* because it makes the meeting too long and causes the subordinates to lose interest in the new project
    D. *advisable* because it gives you a chance to learn which of your subordinates are paying attention to what you say

12. As a supervisor, you are responsible for seeing to it that absenteeism does not become a problem among your subordinates.
    Which one of the following is NOT an acceptable way of controlling the problem of excessive absences?

    A. Distribute a written statement to your staff on the policies regarding absenteeism in your organization.
    B. Arrange for workers who have the fewest absences to talk to those workers who have the most absences.
    C. Let your subordinates know that a record is being kept of all absences.
    D. Arrange for counseling of those employees who are frequently absent.

13. One of your supervisors has been an excellent worker for the past two years. There are no promotion opportunities for this worker in the forseeable future. Due to the city's present budget crisis, a salary increase is not possible.
    Under the circumstances, which one of the following actions on your part would be MOST likely to continue to motivate this worker?

    A. Tell the worker that times are bad all over and jobs are hard to find.
    B. Give the worker less work and easier assignments.
    C. Tell the worker to try to look for a better paying job elsewhere.
    D. Seek the worker's advice often and show that the suggestions provided are appreciated.

14. As a supervisor in a warehouse, it is important that you use your available work force to its fullest potential. Which one of the following actions on your part is MOST likely to increase the effectiveness of your work force?

    A. Assigning more workers to a job than the number actually needed.
    B. Eliminating all job training to allow more time for work output.
    C. Using your best workers on jobs that average workers can do.
    D. Making sure that all materials and equipment used are maintained in good working order.

15. You learn that your storage area will soon be undergoing changes which will affect the work of your subordinates. You decide not to tell your subordinates about what is to happen.
    Of the following, your action can BEST be described as

    A. *wise* because your subordinates will learn of the changes for themselves
    B. *unwise* because your subordinates should be advised about what is to happen
    C. *wise* because it is better for your subordinates to continue working without being disturbed by such news
    D. *unwise* because the work of your subordinates will gradually slow down

16. In making plans for the operation of your unit, you are MOST likely to see these plans carried out successfully if you

    A. allow your staff to participate in developing these plans
    B. do not spend any time on the minor details of these plans
    C. base these plans on the past experiences of others
    D. allow these plans to interact with outside activities in other units

17. A colorless, odorless, and toxic gas that is contained in the exhausts of almost all internal combustion engines is

    A. nitrogen
    B. oxygen
    C. carbon monoxide
    D. sulphur dioxide

18. According to the New York City Fire Code, the recommended clearance from the top of stored warehouse goods to the sprinkler heads must be a minimum of _____ inches.

    A. 2   B. 6   C. 12   D. 18

19. According to the City Fire Code, the recommended width of aisle space in a storage area must be a minimum of _____ foot(feet).

    A. 1   B. 2   C. 3   D. 4

20. As a supervisor in charge of the total operation of a food supply warehouse, you find vandalism to be a potentially serious problem. On occasion, trespassers have gained entrance into the facility by climbing over an unprotected 8-foot fence surrounding the warehouse whose dimensions measure 100 feet by 100 feet.
    Assuming that all of the following would be equally effective ways in preventing these breaches in security in the situation described above, which one would be LEAST costly?

    A. Using two trained guard dogs to roam freely throughout the facility at night.
    B. Hiring a security guard to patrol the facility after working hours.
    C. Installing tape razor wire on top of the fence surrounding the facility.
    D. Installing an electronic burglar alarm system requiring the installation of a new fence.

21. Assume that you are considering training one of your subordinates, Mr. Parks, to help you with your record keeping duties. You have decided on using the following four steps in your instruction:
    I. Show Mr. Parks what has to be done.
    II. Find out what Mr. Parks knows about the job.
    III. Check to see how Mr. Parks is doing the job.
    IV. Have Mr. Parks do the job himself.
    Which one of the following shows the order of taking these steps that would be MOST effective in training Mr. Parks?

    A. II, I, IV, III
    B. III, II, I, IV
    C. I, IV, III, II
    D. IV, I, II, III

22. The one of the following which provides for efficient storage of loose hardware items such as nails, screws, nuts, bolts, and washers is a(n)

    A. wire mesh basket
    B. metal stack bin
    C. open shelf unit
    D. 55-gallon drum

23. A pallet load template is used to

    A. construct new pallets
    B. determine the floor load capacity in a warehouse
    C. determine the size of the pallet needed for different-sized cartons
    D. increase the allowable floor load in a warehouse

24. The fire extinguisher which is a pump-type tank water unit is used for fires involving all of the following EXCEPT

    A. wood   B. paper   C. plastic   D. grease

25. When storing 55-gallon drums outdoors, it is BEST to place the drums on their sides in order to

    A. make them easier to store
    B. prevent rain water from collecting on their tops
    C. allow them to be stacked higher
    D. keep the aisle space smaller

26. In the storage of a flammable liquid, the vapor density of the liquid is the MOST important factor in determining the

    A. type of fire extinguisher to use
    B. type of container used for storage
    C. location of the ventilating outlets
    D. usable life of a product

27. Of the following, the BEST place to store partially loaded pallets is

    A. under fully loaded pallets
    B. over other partially loaded pallets
    C. on the top of stacked pallets
    D. in the aisle space between two rows of stacked pallets

28. Of the following, the BEST reason why there should be a clearance on all sides of a stack of loaded pallets is to prevent the

    A. tipping of the stack
    B. crushing of the lower pallets
    C. collection of moisture in between the stacks
    D. dislocation of the surrounding stacks

29. Where forklift equipment is available, dunnage strips are MOST useful for which one of the following?

    A. Storing a variety of stock items on loaded pallets
    B. Stacking large containers, boxes, and crates
    C. Storing pipes or other round items
    D. Stacking items to be stored on shelves for a long time

30. Of the following, the MAIN advantage in the use of an *A* frame storage rack is that it provides

    A. storage space for extremely large supplies of any item
    B. storage space for any item that is to be shipped out immediately
    C. a quick access to items that have to be inspected
    D. maximum accessibility to smaller lots of bulk supplies

31. Which one of the following can be used to provide an efficient means of storing and stacking items that do not readily lend themselves to direct stacking?
A

   A. pallet spear
   B. collapsible pallet box
   C. skid
   D. two-way entry pallet

32. Of the following, the MAJOR benefit of good housekeeping in a warehouse is that it

   A. allows workers more time to perform their regular duties
   B. reduces the need for fire prevention and safety precautions
   C. conserves space, equipment, time, and effort
   D. reduces the need for identifying stock items and storage areas

33. Which one of the following is a good warehouse practice when receiving goods which will require inspection and tests?

   A. Put the goods aside and have them properly labelled.
   B. Leave the goods on the loading dock.
   C. Place the goods into stock without delay.
   D. Issue the goods to the user.

34. The one of the following which is a MAJOR advantage of a power-driven belt conveyor over a gravity-roller conveyor is that a power-driven belt conveyor can

   A. be operated manually with equal effectiveness
   B. move loads from a lower level to a higher level
   C. be operated at any angle
   D. be easily extended by adding sections

35. Of the following, the PRIMARY purpose for using pallets in handling stock is to provide

   A. a large floor load capacity in a warehouse
   B. easy storage of irregular items in a warehouse
   C. efficient handling and storing of material in a warehouse
   D. a safe working environment in a warehouse

36. Of the following, the FIRST consideration in determining whether a particular piece of materials handling equipment should be purchased for use in a large warehouse is the

   A. qualifications of the personnel using the equipment
   B. reliability of the manufacturer
   C. availability of the replacement parts
   D. allowable floor load capacity

37. When a shipment of goods is made to a warehouse, the person receiving the shipment should check the shipment against the freight bill or bill of lading.
The one of the following that thr receiver should note and sign for on the freight bill or bill of lading is the

   A. size of the packages in the shipment
   B. overage, shortage, or damage to the goods
   C. outside identification on the packages
   D. remaining number of shipments to be made

38. In planning how to handle the receipt of goods from a vendor efficiently, which one of the following would be the MOST useful information to have?
The

    A. unit price of the goods to be delivered
    B. cost for shipping the goods
    C. estimated time of arrival and the size of the delivery
    D. type of material used in packing the goods

39. A using agency has just notified you that they will no longer be using a certain item due to changes in the agency's functions. There is a large supply of this item on hand in your warehouse, and two routine shipments are due next month from the vendor.
Of the following, the MOST advisable action for you to take FIRST in this situation is to

    A. determine if other city warehouses can use these supplies
    B. store the supplies in an inactive section of the warehouse
    C. prepare relinquishment forms to remove existing supplies for resale by the city
    D. notify the proper authority to cancel any orders not yet received

40. A decision has been made to computerize your warehouse inventory control operation. Upon receiving your first computer readout, you notice that it indicates a shortage of a stock item that is usually in good supply.
Of the following, the FIRST step you should take to deal with this matter is to

    A. make a report of a possible theft
    B. report to the computer center that they are in error
    C. verify the information used for the computer readout
    D. request that the computer be repaired

KEY (CORRECT ANSWERS)

1. B	11. B	21. A	31. A
2. C	12. B	22. B	32. C
3. C	13. D	23. C	33. A
4. B	14. D	24. D	34. B
5. C	15. B	25. B	35. C
6. B	16. A	26. C	36. D
7. D	17. C	27. C	37. B
8. A	18. D	28. D	38. C
9. B	19. C	29. B	39. D
10. A	20. C	30. D	40. C

SUPERVISION, ADMINISTRATION, MANAGEMENT AND ORGANIZATION
EXAMINATION SECTION
TEST 1

DIRECTIONS: Each question or incomplete statement is followed by several suggested answers or completions. Select the one that BEST answers the question or completes the statement. *PRINT THE LETTER OF THE CORRECT ANSWER IN THE SPACE AT THE RIGHT.*

1. The one of the following practices by a supervisor which is MOST likely to lead to confusion and inefficiency is for him to
   A. give orders verbally directly to the man assigned to the job
   B. issue orders only in writing
   C. follow up his orders after issuing them
   D. relay his orders to the men through co-workers

   1._____

2. If you are given an oral order by a supervisor which you do not understand completely, you should
   A. use your own judgment
   B. discuss the order with your men
   C. ask your supervisor for a further explanation
   D. carry out that part of the order which you do understand and then ask for more information

   2._____

3. An orientation program for a group of new employees should NOT ordinarily include a
   A. review of the organizational structure of the agency
   B. detailed description of the duties of each new employee
   C. description of the physical layout of the repair shop
   D. statement of the rules pertaining to sick leave, vacation, and holidays

   3._____

4. The MOST important rule to follow with regard to discipline is that a man should be disciplined
   A. after everyone has had time to "cool off"
   B. as soon as possible after the infraction of rules
   C. only for serious rule violations
   D. before he makes a mistake

   4._____

5. If the men under your supervision continue to work effectively even when you are out sick for several days, it would MOST probably indicate that
   A. the men are merely trying to show you up
   B. the men are in constant fear of you and are glad you are away
   C. you have trained your men properly and have their full cooperation
   D. you are serving no useful purpose since the men can get along without you

   5._____

6. When evaluating subordinates, the employee who should be rated HIGHEST by his supervisor is the one who
   A. never lets the supervisor do heavy lifting
   B. asks many questions about the work
   C. makes many suggestions on work procedures
   D. listens to instructions and carries them out

7. Of the following, the factor which is generally MOST important to the conduct of successful training is
   A. time   B. preparation   C. equipment   D. space

8. One of the MAJOR disadvantages of "on-the-job" training is that it
   A. requires a long training period for instructors
   B. may not be progressive
   C. requires additional equipment
   D. may result in the waste of supplies

9. For a supervisor to train workers in several trades which involve various skills, presents many training problems.
   The one of the following which is NOT true in such a training situation is that
   A. less supervision is required
   B. greater planning for training is required
   C. rotation of assignments is necessary
   D. less productivity can be expected

10. For a supervisor of repair workers to have each worker specialize in learning a single trade is GENERALLY
    A. *desirable*; each worker will become expert in his assigned trade
    B. *undesirable*; there is less flexibility of assignments possible when each worker has learned only a single trade
    C. *desirable*; the training responsibility of the supervisor is simplified when each worker is required to learn a single trade
    D. *undesirable*; workers lose interest quickly when they know they are expected to learn a single trade

11. An IMPORTANT advantage of standardizing work procedures is that it
    A. develops all-around skills
    B. makes the work less monotonous
    C. provides an incentive for good work
    D. enable the work to be done with less supervision

12. Generally, the GREATEST difficulty in introducing new work methods is due to the fact that
    A. men become set in their ways
    B. the old way is generally better
    C. only the department will benefit from changes
    D. explaining new methods is time consuming

13. Assume that you are required to transmit an order with, which you do not agree, to your subordinates.
    In this case, it would be BEST for you to
    A. ask one of your superiors to transmit the order
    B. refuse to transmit an order with which you do not agree
    C. transmit the order but be sure to explain that you do not agree with it
    D. transmit the order and enforce it to the best of your ability

14. The MAIN reason for written orders is that
    A. proper blame can be placed if the order is not carried out
    B. the order will be carried out faster
    C. the order can be properly analyzed as to its meaning
    D. there will be no doubt as to what the order says

15. You have been informed unofficially by another shop manager that some of the men under your supervision are loafing on the job.
    This situation can be BEST handled by
    A. telling the man to mind his own business
    B. calling the men together and reprimanding them
    C. having the men work under your direct supervision
    D. arranging to make spot checks at more frequent intervals

16. Suggestions on improving methods of doing work, when submitted by a new employee, should be
    A. examined for possible merit because the new man may have a fresh viewpoint
    B. ignored because it would make the old employees resentful
    C. disregarded because he is too unfamiliar with the work
    D. examined only for the purpose of judging the new man

17. One of your employees often slows down the work of his crew by playing practical jokes.
    The BEST way to handle this situation is to
    A. arrange for his assignment to more than his share of unpleasant jobs
    B. warn him that he must stop this practice at once
    C. ignore this situation for he will soon tire of it
    D. ask your supervisor to transfer him

18. One of your men is always complaining about working conditions, equipment, and his fellow workers.
    The BEST action for you to take in this situation is to
    A. have this man work alone if possible
    B. consider each complaint on is merits
    C. tell him bluntly that you will not listen to any of his complaints
    D. give this man the worst jobs until he quits complaining

19. It is generally agreed that men who are interested in their work will do the best work.
    A supervisor can LEAST stimulate this interest by
    A. complimenting men on good work
    B. correcting men on their working procedures
    C. striving to create overtime for his men
    D. recommending merit raises for excellent work

20. If you, as a supervisor, have criticized one of your men for making a mistake, you should
    A. remind the man of his error from time to time to keep him on his toes
    B. overlook any further errors which this man may make, otherwise he may feel he is a victim of discrimination
    C. give the man the opportunity to redeem himself
    D. impress the man with the fact that all his work will be closely checked from then on

21. In his efforts to maintain standards of performance, a shop manager uses a system of close supervision to detect or catch errors.
    An *opposite* method of accomplishing the *same* objective is to employ a program which
    A. instills in each employee a pride of workmanship to do the job correctly the first time
    B. groups each job accordingly to the importance to the overall objectives of the program
    C. makes the control of quality the responsibility of an inspector
    D. emphasizes that there is a "one" best way for an employee to do s specific job

22. Assume that after taking over a repair shop, a shop manager feels that he is taking too much time maintaining records.
    He should
    A. temporarily assign this job to one of his senior repair crew chiefs
    B. get together with his supervisor to determine if all these records are needed
    C. stop keeping those records which he believes are unnecessary
    D. spend a few additional hours each day until his records are current

23. In order to apply performance standards to employees engaged in repair shop activities, a shop manager must FIRST
    A. allow workers to decide for themselves the way to do the job
    B. determine what is acceptable as satisfactory work
    C. separate the more difficult tasks from the simpler tasks
    D. stick to an established work schedule

24. Of the following actions a shop manager can take to determine whether the vehicles used in his shop are being utilized properly, the one which will give him the LEAST meaningful information is
    A. conducting an analysis of vehicle assignments
    B. reviewing the number of miles traveled by each vehicle with and without loads
    C. recording the unloaded weights of each vehicle
    D. comparing the amount of time vehicles are parked at job sites with the time required to travel to and from job sites

25. For a shop manager, the MOST important reason that equipment which is used infrequently should be considered for disposal is that
    A. the time required for its maintenance could be better used elsewhere
    B. such equipment may cause higher management to think that your shop is not busy
    C. the men may resent having to work on such equipment
    D. such equipment usually has a higher breakdown rate in operation

KEY (CORRECT ANSWERS)

1.	D	11.	D
2.	C	12.	A
3.	B	13.	D
4.	B	14.	D
5.	C	15.	D
6.	D	16.	A
7.	B	17.	B
8.	B	18.	B
9.	A	19.	C
10.	B	20.	C

21.	A
22.	B
23.	B
24.	C
25.	A

TEST 2

DIRECTIONS: Each question or incomplete statement is followed by several suggested answers or completions. Select the one that BEST answers the question or completes the statement. *PRINT THE LETTER OF THE CORRECT ANSWER IN THE SPACE AT THE RIGHT.*

1. Assume that one of your subordinates approaches you with a grievance concerning working conditions.
   Of the following, the BEST action for you to take first is to
   A. "soft-soap" him, since most grievances are imaginary
   B. settle the grievance to his satisfaction
   C. try to talk him out of his complaint
   D. listen patiently and sincerely to the complaint

   1.____

2. Of the following, the BEST way for a supervisor to help a subordinate learn a new skill which requires the use of tools is for him to give this subordinate
   A. a list of good books on the subject
   B. lectures on the theoretical aspects of the task
   C. opportunities to watch someone using the tools
   D. opportunities to practice the skill, under close supervision

   2.____

3. A supervisor finds that his own work load is excessive because several of his subordinates are unable to complete their assignments.
   Of the following, the BEST action for him to take to improve this situation is to
   A. discipline these subordinates
   B. work overtime
   C. request additional staff
   D. train these subordinates in more efficient work methods

   3.____

4. The one of the following situations which is MOST likely to be the result of *poor* morale is a(n)
   A. high rate of turnover
   B. decrease in number of requests by subordinates for transfers
   C. increase in the backlog of work
   D. decrease in the rate of absenteeism

   4.____

5. As a supervisor, you find that several of your subordinates are not meeting their deadlines because they are doing work assigned to them by one of your fellow supervisors without your knowledge.
   Of the following, the BEST course of action for you to take in this situation is to
   A. tell the other supervisors to make future assignments through you
   B. assert your authority by publicly telling the other supervisors to stop issuing orders to your workers
   C. go along with this practice; it is an effective way to fully utilize the available manpower
   D. take the matter directly to your immediate supervisor without delay

   5.____

6. If a supervisor of a duplicating section in an agency hears a rumor concerning a change in agency personnel policy through the "grapevine," he should
   A. *repeat* it to his subordinates so they will be informed
   B. *not repeat* it to his subordinates before he determines the facts because, as supervisor, his work may give it unwarranted authority
   C. *repeat* it to his subordinates so that they will like him for confiding in them
   D. *not repeat* it to his subordinates before he determines the facts because a duplicating section is not concerned with matters of policy

6._____

7. When teaching a new employee how to operate a machine, a supervisor should FIRST
   A. let the employee try to operate the machine by himself, since he can learn only by his mistakes
   B. explain the process to him with the use of diagrams before showing him the machine
   C. have him memorize the details of the operation from the manual
   D. explain and demonstrate the various steps in the process, making sure he understands each step

7._____

8. If a subordinate accuses you of always giving him the least desirable assignments, you should IMMEDIATELY
   A. tell him that it is not true and you do not want to hear any more about it
   B. try to get specific details from him, so that you can find out what his impressions are based on
   C. tell him that you distribute assignments in the fairest way possible and he must be mistaken
   D. ask him what current assignment he has that he does not like, and assign it to someone else

8._____

9. Suppose that the production of an operator under your supervision has been unsatisfactory and you have decided to have a talk with him about it.
During the interview, it would be BEST for you to
   A. discuss only the subordinate's weak points so that he can overcome them
   B. discuss only the subordinate's strong points so that he will not become discouraged
   C. compare the subordinate's work with that of his co-workers so that he will know what is expected of him
   D. discuss both his weak and strong points so that he will get a view of his overall performance

9._____

10. Suppose that an operator under your supervision makes a mistake in color on a 2,000-page job and runs it on white paper instead of on blue paper.
Of the following, your BEST course in these circumstances would be to point out the error to the operator and
   A. have the operator rerun the job immediately on blue paper
   B. send the job to the person who ordered it without comment
   C. send the job to the person who ordered it and tell him it could not be done on blue paper
   D. ask the person who ordered the job whether the white paper is acceptable

10._____

11. Assuming that all your subordinates have equal technical competence, the BEST policy for a supervisor to follow when making assignments of undesirable jobs would be to
    A. distribute them as evenly as possible among his subordinates
    B. give them to the subordinate with the poorest attendance record
    C. ask the subordinate with the least seniority to do them
    D. assign them to the subordinate who is least likely to complain

11.____

12. To get the BEST results when training a number of subordinates at the same time, a supervisor should
    A. treat all of them in an identical manner to avoid accusations of favoritism
    B. treat them all fairly, but use different approaches in dealing with people of different personality types
    C. train only one subordinate, and have him train the others, because this will save a lot of the supervisor's time
    D. train first the subordinates who learn quickly so as to make the others think that the operation is easy to learn

12.____

13. Assume that, after a week's vacation, you return to find that one of your subordinates has produced a job which is unsatisfactory.
    Your BEST course of action at that time would be to
    A. talk to your personnel department about implementing disciplinary action
    B. discuss unsatisfactory work in the unit at a meeting with all of your subordinates
    C. discuss the job with the subordinate to determine why he was unable to do it properly
    D. ignore the matter, because it is too late to correct the mistake

13.____

14. Suppose that an operator under your supervision informs you that Mr. Y, a senior administrator in your agency, has been submitting for copying many papers which are obviously personal in nature. The operator wants to know what to do about it, since the duplication of personal papers is against agency rules.
    Your BEST course of action in these circumstances would be to
    A. tell the operator to pretend not to notice the content of the material and continue to copy whatever is given to him
    B. tell the operator that Mr. Y, as a senior administrator, must have gotten special permission to have personal papers duplicated
    C. have the operator refer Mr. Y to you and inform Mr. Y yourself that duplication of personal papers is against agency rules
    D. call Mr. Y's superior and tell him that Mr. Y has been having personal papers duplicated, which is against agency rules

14.____

15. Assume that you are teaching a certain process to an operator under your supervision.
    In order to BEST determine whether he is actually learning what you are teaching, you should ask questions which
    A. can easily be answered by a "yes" or "no"
    B. require or encourage guessing

15.____

C. require a short description of what has been taught
D. are somewhat ambiguous so as to make the learner think about the procedures in question

16. If an employee is chronically late or absent, as his supervisor, it would be BEST for you to
    A. let his work pile up so he can see that no one else will do it for him
    B. discuss the matter with him and stress the importance of finding a solution
    C. threaten to enter a written report on the matter into his personnel file
    D. work out a system with him so he can have a different work schedule than the other employees

16._____

17. Assume that you have a subordinate who has just finished a basic training course in the operation of a machine.
    Giving him a large and difficult FIRST assignment would be
    A. *good*, because it would force him to "learn the ropes"
    B. *bad*, because he would probably have difficulty in carrying it out, discouraging him and resulting in a waste of time and supplies
    C. *good*, because how he handles it would give you an excellent basis for judging his competence
    D. *bad*, because he would probably assume that you are discriminating against him

17._____

18. After putting a new employee under your supervision through an initial training period, assigning him to work with a more experienced employee for a while would be a
    A. *good* idea, because it would give him the opportunity to observe what he had been taught and to participate in production himself
    B. *bad* idea, because he should not be required to work under the direction of anyone who is not his supervisor
    C. *good* idea, because it would raise the morale of the more experienced employee who could use him to do all the unpleasant chores
    D. *bad* idea, because the best way for him to learn would be to give him full responsibility for assignments right away

18._____

19. Assume that a supervisor is responsible for ordering supplies for the duplicating section in his agency.
    Which one of the following actions would be MOST helpful in determining when to place orders so that an adequate supply of materials will be on hand at all times?
    A. Taking an inventory of supplies on hand at least every two months
    B. Asking his subordinates to inform him when they see that supplies are low
    C. Checking the inventory of supplies whenever he has time
    D. Keeping a running inventory of supplies and a record of estimated needs

19._____

20. Routine procedures that have worked well in the past should be reviewed periodically by a supervisor MAINLY because
    A. they may have become outdated or in need of revision
    B. employees might dislike the procedures even though they have proven successful in the past
    C. these reviews are the main part of a supervisor's job
    D. this practice serves to give the supervisor an idea of how productive his subordinates are

21. Assume that an employee tells his supervisor about a grievance he has against a co-worker. The supervisor assures the employee that he will immediately take action to eliminate the grievance.
    The supervisor's attitude should be considered
    A. *correct*, because a good supervisor is one who can come to a quick decision
    B. *incorrect*, because the supervisor should have told the employee that he will investigate the grievance and then determine a future course of action
    C. *correct*, because the employee's morale will be higher, resulting in greater productivity
    D. *incorrect*, because the supervisor should remain uninvolved and let the employees settle grievances between themselves

22. If an employee's work output is low and of poor quality due to faulty work habits, the MOST constructive of the following ways for a supervisor to correct this situation generally is to
    A. discipline the employee
    B. transfer the employee to another unit
    C. provide additional training
    D. check the employee's work continuously

23. Assume that it becomes necessary for a supervisor to ask his staff to work overtime.
    Which one of the following techniques is MOST likely to win their willing cooperation to do this?
    A. Explain that this is part of their job specification entitled, "performs related work"
    B. Explain the reason it is necessary for the employees to work overtime
    C. Promise the employees special consideration regarding future leave matters
    D. Explain that if the employees do not work overtime, they will face possible disciplinary action

24. If an employee's work performance has recently fallen below established minimum standards for quality and quantity, the threat of demotion or other disciplinary measures as an attempt to improve this employee's performance would probably be the MOST acceptable and effective course of action
    A. *only* after other more constructive measures have failed
    B. *if* applied uniformly to all employees as soon as performance falls below standard

25. If, as a supervisor, it becomes necessary for you to assign an employee to supervise your unit during your vacation, it would generally be BEST to select the employee who
    A. is the best technician on the staff
    B. can get the work out smoothly, without friction
    C. has the most seniority
    D. is the most popular with the group

25.____

KEY (CORRECT ANSWERS)

1. D
2. D
3. D
4. A
5. A

6. B
7. D
8. B
9. D
10. D

11. A
12. B
13. C
14. C
15. C

16. B
17. B
18. A
19. D
20. A

21. B
22. C
23. B
24. A
25. B

TEST 3

DIRECTIONS: Each question or incomplete statement is followed by several suggested answers or completions. Select the one that BEST answers the question or completes the statement. *PRINT THE LETTER OF THE CORRECT ANSWER IN THE SPACE AT THE RIGHT.*

1. An employee under your supervision has demonstrated a deep-seated personality problem that has begun to affect his work.
   This situation should be
   A. *ignored*, mainly because such problems usually resolve themselves
   B. *handled*, mainly because the employee should be assisted in seeking professional help
   C. *ignored*, mainly because the employee will consider any advice as interference
   D. *handled*, mainly because the supervisors should be qualified to resolve deep-seated personality problems

1.____

2. Of the following, a supervisor will usually be MOST successful in maintaining employee morale while providing effective leadership if he
   A. takes prompt disciplinary action every time it is needed
   B. gives difficult assignments only to those workers who ask for such work
   C. promises his workers anything reasonable they request
   D. relies entirely on his staff for decisions

2.____

3. When a supervisor makes an assignment to his subordinates, he should include a clear statement of what results are expected when the assignment is completed.
   Of the following, the BEST reason for following this procedure is that it will
   A. make it unnecessary for the supervisor to check on the progress of the work
   B. stimulate initiative and cooperation on the part of the more responsible workers
   C. give the subordinates a way to judge whether their work is meeting the requirements
   D. give the subordinates the feeling that they have some freedom of action

3.____

4. Assume that, on a new employee's first day of work, his supervisor gives him a good orientation by telling him the general regulations and procedures used in the office and introducing him to his department head and fellow employees.
   For the remainder of the day, it would be BEST for the supervisor to
   A. give him steady instruction in all phases of his job, while stressing its most important aspects
   B. have him observe a fellow employee perform the duties of the job
   C. instruct him in that part of the job which he would prefer to learn first
   D. give him a simple task which requires little instruction and allows him to familiarize himself with the surroundings

4.____

5. When it becomes necessary to criticize subordinates because several errors in the unit's work have been discovered, the supervisor should USUALLY
   A. focus on the job operation and avoid placing personal blame
   B. make every effort to fix blame and admonish the person responsible
   C. include in the criticism those employees who recognize and rectify their own mistakes
   D. repeat the criticism at regular intervals in order to impress the subordinates with the seriousness of their errors

6. If two employees under your supervision are continually bickering and cannot get along together, the FIRST action that you should take is to
   A. investigate possible ways of separating them
   B. ask your immediate superior for the procedure to follow in this situation
   C. determine the cause of their difficulty
   D. develop a plan and tell both parties to try it

7. In general, it is appropriate to recommend the transfer of an employee for all of the following reasons EXCEPT
   A. rewarding him
   B. providing him with a more challenging job
   C. remedying an error in initial placement
   D. disciplining him

8. Of the following, the MAIN disadvantage of basing a training and development program on a series of lectures is that the lecture technique
   A. does not sufficiently involve trainees in the learning process
   B. is more costly than other methods of training
   C. cannot be used to facilitate the understanding of difficult information
   D. is time consuming and inefficient

9. A supervisor has been assigned to train a new employee who is properly motivated but has made many mistakes.
   In the interview between the supervisor and employee about this problem, the employee should FIRST be
   A. asked if he can think of anything that he can do to improve his work
   B. complimented sincerely on some aspect of his work that is satisfactory
   C. asked to explain why he made the mistake
   D. advised that he may be dismissed if he continues to be careless

10. In training subordinates for more complex work, a supervisor must be aware of the progress that the subordinates are making.
    Determination of the results that have been accomplished by training is a concept commonly known as
    A. reinforcement   B. feedback
    C. cognitive dissonance   D. the halo effect

11. Assume that one of your subordinates loses interest in his work because he feels that your recent evaluation of his performance was unfair.
    The one of the following which is the BEST way to help him is to
    A. establish frequent deadlines for his work
    B. discuss his feelings and attitude with him
    C. discuss with him only the positive aspects of his performance
    D. arrange for his transfer to another unit

12. Informal organizations often develop at work.
    Of the following, the supervisor should realize that these groups will USUALLY
    A. determine work pace through unofficial agreements
    B. restrict vital communication channels
    C. lower morale by providing a chance to spread grievances
    D. provide leaders who will substitute for the supervisor when he is absent

13. Assume that you, the supervisor, have called to your office a subordinate whom, on several recent occasions, you have seen using the office telephone for personal use.
    In this situation, it would be MOST appropriate to begin the interview by
    A. discussing the disciplinary action that you believe to be warranted
    B. asking the subordinate to explain the reason for his personal use of the office telephone
    C. telling the subordinate about other employees who were disciplined for the same offense
    D. informing the subordinate that he is not to use the office telephone under any circumstances until further notice

14. Of the following, the success of any formal training program depends PRIMARILY upon the
    A. efficient and thorough preparation of materials, facilities, and procedures for instruction
    B. training program's practical relevance to the on-the-job situation
    C. scheduling of training sessions so as to minimize interference with normal job responsibilities
    D. creation of a positive initial reception on the part of the trainees

15. All of the following are legitimate purposes for regularly evaluating employee performance EXCEPT
    A. stimulating improvement in performance
    B. developing more accurate standards to be used in future ratings
    C. encouraging a spirit of competition
    D. allowing the employee to set realistic work goals for himself

16. A certain supervisor is very conscientious. He wants to receive personally all reports, correspondence, etc., and to be completely involved in all of the unit's operations. However, he is having difficulty in keeping up with the growing amount of paperwork.

Of the following, the MOST desirable course of action for him to take is to
A. put in more hours on the job
B. ask for additional office help
C. begin to delegate more of his work
D. inquire of his supervisor if the paperwork is really necessary

17. Assume that you are a supervisor. One of the workers under your supervision expresses his need to speak to you about a client who has been particularly uncooperative in providing information.
The MOST appropriate action for you to take FIRST would be to
A. agree to see the client for the worker in order to get the information
B. advise the worker to try several more times to get the information before he asks you for help
C. tell the worker you will go with him to see the client in order to observe his technique
D. ask the worker some questions in order to determine the type of help he needs in the situation

17.____

18. The supervisor who is MOST likely to achieve a high level of productivity from the professional employees under his supervision is the one who
A. watches their progress continuously
B. provides them with just enough information to carry out their assigned tasks
C. occasionally pitches in and helps them with their work
D. shares with them responsibility for setting work goals

18.____

19. Assume that there has been considerable friction for some time among the workers of a certain unit. The supervisor in charge of this unit becomes aware that the problem is getting serious as shown by increased absenteeism and lateness, loud arguments, etc.
Of the following, the BEST course of action for the supervisor to take FIRST is to
A. have a staff discussion about objectives and problems
B. seek out and penalize the apparent trouble-makers
C. set up and enforce stricter formal rules
D. discipline the next subordinate who causes friction

19.____

20. Assume that an employee under your supervision asks you for some blank paper and pencils to take home to her young grandson who, she says, delights in drawing.
The one of the following actions you SHOULD take is to
A. give her the material she wants and refrain from any comment
B. refuse her request and tell her that the use of office supplies for personal reasons is not proper
C. give her the material but suggest that she buy it next time
D. tell her to take the material herself since you do not want to know anything about the matter

20.____

21. A certain supervisor is given a performance evaluation by his superior. In it he is commended for his method of "delegation," a term that USUALLY refers to the action of
    A. determining the priorities for activities which must be completed
    B. assigning to subordinates some of the duties for which he is responsible
    C. standardizing operations in order to achieve results as close as possible to established goals
    D. dividing the activities necessary to achieve an objective into simple steps

21.____

22. A supervisor is approached by a subordinate who complains that a fellow worker is not assuming his share of the workload and is, therefore, causing more work for others in the office.
Of the following, the MOST appropriate action for the supervisor to take in response to this complaint is to tell the subordinate
    A. that he will look into the matter
    B. to concentrate on his own job and not to worry about others
    C. to discuss the matter with the other worker
    D. that not everyone is capable of working at the same pace

22.____

23. Aside from the formal relationships established by management, informal and unofficial relationships will be developed among the personnel within an organization.
Of the following, the MAIN importance of such informal relationships to the operations of the formal organization is that they
    A. reinforce the basic goals of the formal organization
    B. insure the interchangeability of the personnel within the organization
    C. provide an additional channel of communications within the organization
    D. insure predictability and control of the behavior of members of the organization

23.____

24. The most productive worker in a unit frequently takes overly-long coffee breaks and lunch hours while maintaining his above-average rate of productivity.
Of the following, it would be MOST advisable for the supervisor to
    A. reprimand him, because rules must be enforced equally regardless of the merit of an individual's job performance
    B. ignore the infractions because a superior worker should be granted extra privileges for his efforts
    C. take no action unless others in the unit complain, because a reprimand may hurt the superior worker's feelings and cause him to produce less
    D. tell other members of the unit that a comparable rate of productivity on their part will be rewarded with similar privileges

24.____

25. A supervisor has been asked by his superior to choose an employee to supervise a special project.
Of the following, the MOST significant factor to consider in making this choice is the employee's
   A. length of service
   B. ability to do the job
   C. commitment to the goals of the agency
   D. attitude toward his fellow workers

25._____

KEY (CORRECT ANSWERS)

1. B
2. A
3. C
4. D
5. A

6. C
7. D
8. A
9. B
10. B

11. B
12. A
13. B
14. B
15. C

16. C
17. D
18. D
19. A
20. B

21. B
22. A
23. C
24. A
25. B

TEST 4

DIRECTIONS: Each question or incomplete statement is followed by several suggested answers or completions. Select the one that BEST answers the question or completes the statement. *PRINT THE LETTER OF THE CORRECT ANSWER IN THE SPACE AT THE RIGHT.*

1. Assume that you are a newly appointed supervisor.
   Your MOST important responsibility is to
   A. make certain that all of the employees under your supervision are treated equally
   B. reduce disciplinary situations to a minimum
   C. insure an atmosphere of mutual trust between your workers and yourself
   D. see that the required work is done properly

   1.____

2. In order to make sure that work is completed on time, the supervisor should
   A. pitch in and do as much of the work herself as she can
   B. schedule the work and control its progress
   C. not assign more than one person to any one task
   D. assign the same amount of work to each subordinate

   2.____

3. Assume that you are a supervisor in charge of a number of workers who do the same kind of work and who each produce about the same volume of work in a given period of time.
   When their performance is evaluated, the worker who should be rated as the MOST accurate is the one
   A. whose errors are the easiest to correct
   B. whose errors involve the smallest amount of money
   C. who makes the fewest errors in her work
   D. who makes fewer errors as she becomes more experienced

   3.____

4. As a supervisor, you have been asked by the manager to recommend whether the work of the bookkeeping office requires a permanent increase in bookkeeping office staff.
   Of the following questions, the one whose answer would be MOST likely to assist you in making your recommendation is:
   A. Are temporary employees hired to handle seasonal fluctuations in work loads?
   B. Are some permanent employees working irregular hours because they occasionally work overtime?
   C. Are the present permanent employees keeping the work of the bookkeeping office current?
   D. Are employees complaining that the work is unevenly divided?

   4.____

5. Assume that you are a supervisor. One of your subordinates tells you that he is dissatisfied with his work assignment and that he wishes to discuss the matter with you. The employee is obviously very angry and upset.
   Of the following, the course of action that you should take FIRST in this situation is to
   A. promise the employee that you will review all the work assignments in the office to determine whether any changes should be made.
   B. have the employee present his complaint, correcting him whenever he makes what seems to be an erroneous charge against you
   C. postpone discussion of the employee's complaint, explaining to him that the matter can be settled more satisfactory if it is discussed calmly
   D. permit the employee to present his complaint in full, withholding your comments until he has finished making his complaint

6. Assume that you are a supervisor. You find that you are spending too much time on routine tasks and not enough time on supervision of the work of your subordinates.
   It would be ADVISABLE for you to
   A. assign some of the routine tasks to your subordinates
   B. postpone the performance of routine tasks until you have completed your supervisory tasks
   C. delegate the supervisory work to a capable subordinate
   D. eliminate some of the supervisory tasks that you are required to perform

7. Assume that you are a supervisor. You discover that one of your workers has violated an important rule.
   The FIRST course of action for you as the supervisor to take would be to
   A. call a meeting of the entire staff and discuss the matter generally without mentioning any employee by name
   B. arrange to supervise the offending worker's activities more closely
   C. discuss the violation privately with the worker involved
   D. discuss the matter with the worker within hearing of the entire staff so that she will feel too ashamed to commit this violation in the future

8. As a supervisor, you are to prepare a vacation schedule for the bookkeeping office employees.
   The one of the following that is the LEAST important factor for you to consider in setting up this schedule is
   A. seniority   B. vacation preferences of employees
   C. average productivity of the office

9. In assigning a complicated task to a group of subordinates, a certain supervisor does not indicate the specific steps to be followed in performing the assignment, nor does he designate which subordinate is to be responsible for seeing that the task is done on time.

This supervisor's method of assigning the task is MOST likely to result in
- A. confusion among subordinates with consequent delays in work
- B. greater individual effort and self-reliance
- C. assumption of authority by capable subordinates
- D. loss of confidence by subordinates in their ability

10. While you are explaining a new procedure to an employee, she asks you a question about the procedure which you cannot answer.
    The MOST appropriate action for you to take is to
    - A. admit your inability to answer the question and promise to obtain the information
    - B. point out the likelihood of a situation arising which would require an answer to the question
    - C. ask the worker to give her reason for asking the question before you give any further reply
    - D. tell her to inform you immediately should a situation arise requiring an answer to her question

KEY (CORRECT ANSWERS)

1.	D	6.	A
2.	B	7.	C
3.	C	8.	C
4.	C	9.	A
5.	D	10.	A

SUPERVISION STUDY GUIDE

Social science has developed information about groups and leadership in general and supervisor-employee relationships in particular. Since organizational effectiveness is closely linked to the ability of supervisors to direct the activities of employees, these findings are important to executives everywhere.

IS A SUPERVISOR A LEADER?

First-line supervisors are found in all large business and government organizations. They are the men at the base of an organizational hierarchy. Decisions made by the head of the organization reach them through a network of intermediate positions. They are frequently referred to as part of the management team, but their duties seldom seem to support this description.

A supervisor of clerks, tax collectors, meat inspectors, or securities analysts is not charged with budget preparation. He cannot hire or fire the employees in his own unit on his say-so. He does not administer programs which require great planning, coordinating, or decision making.

Then what is he? He is the man who is directly in charge of a group of employees doing productive work for a business or government agency. If the work requires the use of machines, the men he supervises operate them. If the work requires the writing of reports, the men he supervises write them. He is expected to maintain a productive flow of work without creating problems which higher levels of management must solve. But is he a leader?

To carry out a specific part of an agency's mission, management creates a unit, staffs it with a group of employees and designates a supervisor to take charge of them. Management directs what this unit shall do, from time to time changes directions, and often indicates what the group should not do. Management presumably creates status for the supervisor by giving him more pay, a title, and special privileges.

Management asks a supervisor to get his workers to attain organizational goals, including the desired quantity and quality of production. Supposedly, he has authority to enable him to achieve this objective. Management at least assumes that by establishing the status of the supervisor's position, it has created sufficient authority to enable him to achieve these goals— not his goals, nor necessarily the group's, but management's goals.

In addition, supervision includes writing reports, keeping records of membership in a higher-level administrative group, industrial engineering, safety engineering, editorial duties, housekeeping duties, etc. The supervisor as a member of an organizational network, must be responsible to the changing demands of the management above him. At the same time, he must be responsive to the demands of the work group of which he is a member. He is placed in the difficult position of communicating and implementing new decisions, changed programs and revised production quotas for his work group, although he may have had little part in developing them.

It follows, then, that supervision has a special characteristic: achievement of goals, previously set by management, through the efforts of others. It is in this feature of the supervisor's job that we find the role of a leader in the sense of the following definition: *A leader is that person who <u>most</u> effectively influences group activities toward goal setting and goal achievements.*

This definition is broad. It covers both leaders in groups that come together voluntarily and in those brought together through a work assignment in a factory, store, or government agency. In the natural group, the authority necessary to attain goals is determined by the group membership and is granted by them. In the working group, it is apparent that the establishment of a supervisory position creates a predisposition on the part of employees to accept the authority of the occupant of that position. We cannot, however, assume that mere occupation confers authority sufficient to assure the accomplishment of an organization's goals.

Supervision is different, then, from leadership. The supervisor is expected to fulfill the role of leader but without obtaining a grant of authority from the group he supervises. The supervisor is expected to influence the group in the achieving of goals but is often handicapped by having little influence on the organizational process by which goals are set. The supervisor, because he works in an organizational setting, has the burdens of additional organizational duties and restrictions and requirements arising out of the fact that his position is subordinate to a hierarchy of higher-level supervisors. These differences between leadership and supervision are reflected in our definition: *Supervision is basically a leadership role, in a formal organization, which has as its objective the effective influencing of other employees.*

Even though these differences between supervision and leadership exist, a significant finding of experimenters in this field is that supervisors <u>must</u> be leaders to be successful.

The problem is: How can a supervisor exercise leadership in an organizational setting? We might say that the supervisor is expected to be a natural leader in a situation which does not come about naturally. His situation becomes really difficult in an organization which is more eager to make its supervisors into followers rather than leaders.

LEADERSHIP: NATURAL AND ORGANIZATIONAL

Leadership, in its usual sense of *natural* leadership, and supervision are not the same. In some cases, leadership embraces broader powers and functions than supervision; in other cases, supervision embraces more than leadership. This is true both because of the organization and technical aspects of the supervisor's job and because of the relatively freer setting and inherent authority of the natural leader.

The natural leader usually has much more authority and influence than the supervisor. Group members not only follow his command but prefer it that way. The employee, however, can appeal the supervisor's commands to his union or to the supervisor's superior or to the personnel office. These intercessors represent restrictions on the supervisor's power to lead.

The natural leader can gain greater membership involvement in the group's objectives, and he can change the objectives of the group. The supervisor can attempt to gain employee support only for management's objectives; he cannot set other objectives. In these instances leadership is broader than supervision.

The natural leader must depend upon whatever skills are available when seeking to attain objectives. The supervisor is trained in the administrative skills necessary to achieve management's goals. If he does not possess the requisite skills, however, he can call upon management's technicians.

A natural leader can maintain his leadership, in certain groups, merely by satisfying members' need for group affiliation. The supervisor must maintain his leadership by directing and organizing his group to achieve specific organizational goals set for him and his group by management. He must have a technical competence and a kind of coordinating ability which is not needed by many natural leaders.

A natural leader is responsible only to his group which grants him authority. The supervisor is responsible to management, which employs him, and also to the work group of which he is a member. The supervisor has the exceedingly difficult job of reconciling the demands of two groups frequently in conflict. He is often placed in the untenable position of trying to play two antagonistic roles. In the above instance, supervision is broader than leadership.

ORGANIZATIONAL INFLUENCES ON LEADERSHIP

The supervisor is both a product and a prisoner of the organization wherein we find him. The organization which creates the supervisor's position also obstructs, restricts, and channelizes the exercise of his duties. These influences extend beyond prescribed functional relationships to specific supervisory behavior. For example, even in a face-to-face situation involving one of his subordinates, the supervisor's actions are controlled to a great extent by his organization. His behavior must conform to the organization policy on human relations, rules which dictate personnel procedures, specific prohibitions governing conduct, the attitudes of his own superior, etc. He is not a free agent operating within the limits of his work group. His freedom of action is much more circumscribed than is generally admitted. The organizational influences which limit his leadership actions can be classified as structure, prescriptions, and proscriptions.

The organizational structure places each supervisor's position in context with other designated positions. It determines the relationships between his position and specific positions which impinge on his. The structure of the organization designates a certain position to which he looks for orders and information about his work. It gives a particular status to his position within a pattern of statuses from which he perceives that (1) certain positions are on a par, organizationally, with his, (2) other positions are subordinate, and (3) still others are superior.

The organizational structure determines those positions to which he should look for advice and assistance, and those positions to which he should give advice and assistance.

For instance, the organizational structure has predetermined that the supervisor of a clerical processing unit shall report to a supervisory position in a higher echelon. He shall have certain relationships with the supervisors of the work units which transmit work to and receive work from his unit. He shall discuss changes and clarification of procedures with certain staff units, such as organization and methods, cost accounting, and personnel. He shall consult supervisors of units which provide or receive special work assignments.

The organizational structure, however, establishes patterns other than those of the relationships of positions. These are the patterns of responsibility, authority, and expectations.

The supervisor is responsible for certain activities or results; he is presumably invested with the authority to achieve these. His set of authority and responsibility is interwoven with other sets to the end that all goals and functions of the organization are parceled out in small, manageable lots. This, of course, establishes a series of expectations: a single supervisor can perform his particular set of duties only upon the assumption that preceding or contiguous sets of duties have been, or are being carried out. At the same time, he is aware of the expectations of others that he will fulfill his functional role.

The structure of an organization establishes relationships between specified positions and specific expectations for these positions. The fact that these relationships and expectations are established is one thing; whether or not they are met is another.

PRESCRIPTIONS AND PROSCRIPTIONS

But let us return to the organizational influences which act to restrict the supervisor's exercise of leadership. These are the prescriptions and proscriptions generally in effect in all organizations, and those peculiar to a single organization. In brief these are the *thou shalt's* and the *thou shalt not's*.

Organizations not only prescribe certain duties for individual supervisory positions, they also prescribe specific methods and means of carrying out these duties and maintaining management-employee relations. These include rules, regulations, policy, and tradition. It does no good for the supervisor to say, *This seems to be the best way to handle such-and-such,* if the organization has established a routine for dealing with problems. For good or bad, there are rules that state that firings shall be executed in such a manner, accompanied by a certain notification; that training shall be conducted, and in this manner. Proscriptions are merely negative prescriptions; you may not discriminate against any employee because of politics or race; you shall not suspend any employee without following certain procedures and obtaining certain approvals.

Most of these prohibitions and rules apply to the area of interpersonal relations, precisely the area which is now arousing most interest on the part of administrators and managers. We have become concerned about the contrast between formally prescribed relationships and interpersonal relationships, and this brings us to the often discussed informal organization.

FORMAL AND INFORMAL ORGANIZATIONS

As we well know, the functions and activities of any organization are broken down into individual units of work called positions. Administrators must establish a pattern which will link these positions to each other and relate them to a system of authority and responsibility. Man-to-man are spelled out as plainly as possible for all to understand. Managers, then, build an official structure which we call the formal organization.

In these same organizations, employees react individually and in groups to institutionally determined roles. John, a worker, rides in the same carpool as Joe, a foreman. An unplanned communication develops. Harry, a machinist knows more about high-speed machining than his foreman or anyone else in his shop. An unofficial tool boss comes into being. Mary, who fought with Jane, is promoted over her. Jane now gives Mary's directions. A planned relationship fails to develop. The employees have built a structure which we call the informal organization.

> *Formal organization is a system of management-prescribed relations between positions in an organization.*

> *Informal organization is a network of unofficial relations between people in an organization.*

These definitions might lead us to the absurd conclusion that positions carry out formal activities and that employe4es spend their time in unofficial activities. We must recognize that organizational activities are in all cases carried out by people. The formal structure provides a needed framework within which interpersonal relations occur. What we call informal organization is the complex of normal, natural relations among employees. These personal relationships may be negative or positive. That is, they may impede or aid the achievement of organizational goals. For example, friendship between two supervisors greatly increases the probability of good cooperation and coordination between their sections. On the other hand, *buck passing* nullifies the formal structure by failure to meet a prescribed and expected responsibility.

It is improbable that an ideal organization exists where all activities are carried out in strict conformity to a formally prescribed pattern of functional roles. Informal organization arises because of the incompleteness and ambiguities in the network of formally prescribed relationships, or in response to the needs or inadequacies of supervisors or managers who hold prescribed functional roles in an organization. Many of these relationships are not prescribed by the organizational pattern; many cannot be prescribed; many should not be prescribed.

Management faces the problem of keeping the informal organization in harmony with the mission of the agency. One way to do this is to make sure that all employees have a clear understanding of and are sympathetic with that mission. The issuance of organizational charts, procedural manuals, and functional descriptions of the work to be done by divisions and sections helps communicate management's plans and goals. Issuances alone, of course, cannot do the whole job. They should be accompanied by oral discussion and explanation. Management must ensure that there is mutual understanding and acceptance of charts and procedures. More important is that management acquaint itself with the attitudes, activities, and peculiar brands of logic which govern the informal organization. Only through this type of knowledge can they and supervisors keep informal goals consistent with the agency mission.

SUPERVISION STATUS AND FUNCTIONAL ROLE

A well-established supervisor is respected by the employees who work with him. They defer to his wishes. It is clear that a superior-subordinate relationship has been established. That is, status of the supervisor has been established in relation to other employees of the same work group. This same supervisor gains the respect of employees when he behaves in as certain manner. He will be expected, generally, to follow the customs of the group in such matters as dress, recreation, and manner of speaking. The group has a set of expectations as to his behavior. His position is a functional role which carries with it a collection of rights and obligations.

The position of supervisor usually has a status distinct from the individual who occupies it: it is much like a position description which exists whether or not there is an incumbent. The status of a supervisory position is valued higher than that of an employee position both because of the functional role of leadership which is assigned to it and because of the status symbols of titles, rights, and privileges which go with it.

Social ranking, or status, is not simple because it involves both the position and the man. An individual may be ranked higher than others because of his education, social background, perceived leadership ability, or conformity to group customs and ideals. If such a man is ranked higher by the members of a work group than their supervisor, the supervisor's effectiveness may be seriously undermined.

If the organization does not build and reinforce a supervisor's status, his position can be undermined in a different way. This will happen when managers go around rather than through the supervisor or designate him as a straw boss, acting boss, or otherwise not a real boss.

Let us clarify this last point. A role, and corresponding status, establishes a set of expectations. Employees expect their supervisor to do certain things and to act in certain ways. They are prepared to respond to that expected behavior. When the supervisor's behavior does not conform to their expectations, they are surprised, confused, and ill-at-ease. It becomes necessary for them to resolve their confusion, if they can. They might do this by turning to one of their own members for leadership. If the confusion continues, or their attempted solutions are not satisfactory, they will probably become a poorly motivated, non-cohesive group which cannot function very well.

COMMUNICATION AND THE SUPERVISOR

In a recent survey, railroad workers reported that they rarely look to their supervisor for information about the company. This is startling, at least to us, because we ordinarily think of the supervisor as the link between management and worker. We expect the supervisor to be the prime source of information about the company. Actually, the railroad workers listed the supervisor next to last in the o5rder of their sources of information. Most surprising of all, the supervisors, themselves, stated that rumor and unofficial contacts were their principal sources of information. Here we see one of the reasons why supervisors may not be as effective as management desires.

The supervisor is not only being bypassed by his work group, he is being ignored, and his position weakened, by the very organization which is holding him responsible for the activities of his workers. If he is management's representative to the employee, then management has an obligation to keep him informed of its activities. This is necessary if he is to carry out his functions efficiently and maintain his leadership in the work group. The supervisor is expected to be a source of information; when he is not, his status is not clear, and employees are dissatisfied because he has not lived up to expectations.

By providing information to the supervisor to pass along to employees, we can strengthen his position as leader of the group, and increase satisfaction and cohesion within the group. Because he has more information than the other members, receives information sooner, and passes it along at the proper times, members turn to him as a source and also provide him with information in the hope of receiving some in return. From this, we can see an increase in group cohesiveness because:

- Employees are bound closer to their supervisor because he is *in the know*.
- There is less need to go outside the group for answers
- Employees will more quickly turn to the supervisor for enlightenment

The fact that he has the answers will also enhance the supervisor's standing in the eyes of his men. This increased status will serve to bolster his authority and control of the group and will probably result in improved morale and productivity.

The foregoing, of course, does not mean that all management information should be given out. There are obviously certain policy determinations and discussions which need not or cannot be transmitted to all supervisors. However, the supervisor must be kept as fully informed as possible so that he can answer questions when asked and can allay needless fears and anxieties. Further, the supervisor has the responsibility of encouraging employee questions and submissions of information. He must be able to present information to employees so that it is clearly understood and accepted. His attitude and manner should make it clear that he believes in what he is saying, that the information is necessary or desirable to the group, and that he is prepared to act on the basis of the information.

SUPERVISION AND JOB PERFORMANCE

The productivity of work groups is a product; employees' efforts are multiplied by the supervision they receive. Many investigators have analyzed this relationship and have discovered elements of supervision which differentiate high and low production groups. These researchers have identified certain types of supervisory practices which they classify as *employee-centered* and other types which they classify as *production centered*.

The difference between these two kinds of supervision lies not in specific practices but in the approach or orientation to supervision. The employee-centered supervisor directs most of his efforts toward increasing employee motivation. He is concerned more with realizing the potential energy of persons than with administrative and technological methods of increasing efficiency and productivity. He is the man who finds ways of causing employees to want to work harder with the same tools. These supervisors emphasize the personal relations between their employees and themselves.

Now, obviously, these pictures are overdrawn. No one supervisor has all the virtues of the ideal type of employee-centered supervisor. And, fortunately, no one supervisor has all the bad traits found in many production-centered supervisors. We should remember that the various practices that researchers have fond which distinguish these two kinds of supervision represent the many practices and methods of supervisors of all gradations between these extremes. We should be careful, too, of the implications of the labels attached to the two types. For instance, being production-centered is not necessarily bad, since the principal responsibility of any supervisor is maintaining the production level that is expected of his work group. Being employee-centered may not necessarily be good, if the only result is a happy, chuckling crew of loafers. To return to the researchers' findings, employee-centered supervisors:

- Recommend promotions, transfers, pay increases
- Inform men about what is happening in the company
- Keep men posted on how well they are doing
- Hear complaints and grievances sympathetically
- Speak up for subordinates

Production-centered supervisors, on the other hand, don't do those things. They check on employees more frequently, give more detailed and frequent instructions, don't give reasons for changes, and are more punitive when mistakes are made. Employee-centered supervisors were reported to contribute to high morale and high production, whereas production-centered supervision was associated with lower morale and less production.

More recent findings, however, show that the relationship between supervision and productivity is not this simple. Investigators now report that high production is more frequently associated with supervisory practices which combine employee-centered behavior with concern for production. (This concern is not the same, however, as anxiety about production, which is the hallmark of our production-centered supervisor.) Let us examine these apparently contradictory findings and the premises from which they are derived.

SUPERVISION AND MORALE

Why do supervisory activities cause high or low production? As the name implies, the activities of the employee-centered supervisor tend to relate him more closely and satisfactorily to his workers. The production-centered supervisor's practices tend to separate him from his group and to foster antagonism. An analysis of this difference may answer our question.

Earlier, we pointed out that the supervisor is a type of leader and that leadership is intimately related to the group in which it occurs We discover, now, that an employee-centered supervisor's primary activities are concerned with both his leadership and his group membership. Such a supervisor is a member of a group and occupies a leadership role in that group.

These facts are sometimes obscured when we speak of the supervisor as management's representative, or as the organizational link between management and the employee, or as the end of the chain of command. If we really want to understand what it is we expect of the supervisor, we must remember that he is the designated leader of a group of employees to whom he is bound by interaction and interdependence.

Most of his actions are aimed, consciously or unconsciously, at strengthening membership ties in the group. This includes both making members more conscious that he is a member of their group) and causing members to identify themselves more closely with the group. These ends are accomplished by:

- making the group more attractive to the worker: they find satisfaction of their needs for recognition, friendship, enjoyable work, etc.;
- maintaining open communication: employees can express their views and obtain information about the organization
- giving assistance: members can seek advice on personal problems as well as their work; and
- acting as a buffer between the group and management: he speaks up for his men and explains the reasons for management's decisions.

Such actions both strengthen group cohesiveness and solidarity and affirm the supervisor's leadership position in the group.

DEFINING MORALE

This brings us back to a point mentioned earlier. We had said that employee-centered supervisors contribute to high morale as well as to high production. But how can we explain units which have low morale and high productivity, or vice versa? Usually production and morale are considered separately, partly because they are measured against different criteria and partly because, in some instances, they seem to be independent of each other.

Some of this difficulty may stem from confusion over definitions of morale. Morale has been defined as, or measured by, absences from work, satisfaction with job or company, dissension among members of work groups, productivity, apathy or lack of interest, readiness to help others, and a general aura of happiness as rated by observers. Some of these criteria of morale are not subject to the influence of the supervisor, and some of them are not clearly related to productivity. Definitions like these invite findings of low morale coupled with high production.

Both productivity and morale can be influenced by environmental factors not under the control of group members or supervisors. Such things as plant layout, organizational structure and goals, lighting, ventilation, communications, and management planning may have an adverse or desirable effect.

We might resolve the dilemma by defining morale on the basis of our understanding of the supervisor as leader of a group; morale is the degree of satisfaction of group members with their leadership. In this light, the supervisor's employee-centered activities bear a clear relation to morale. His efforts to increase employee identification with the group and to strengthen his leadership lead to greater satisfaction with that leadership. By increasing group cohesiveness and by demonstrating that his influence and power can aid the group, he is able to enhance his leadership status and afford satisfaction to the group.

SUPERVISION, PRODUCTION, AND MORALE

There are factors within the organization itself which determine whether increased production is possible:

- Are production goals expressed in terms understandable to employees and are they realistic?
- Do supervisors responsible for production respect the agency mission and production goals?
- If employees do not know how to do the job well, does management provide a trainer—often the supervisor—who can teach efficient work methods?

There are other factors within the work group which determine whether increased production will be attained:

- Is leadership present which can bring about the desired level of production?
- Are production goals accepted by employees as reasonable and attainable?
- If group effort is involved, are members able to coordinate their efforts?

Research findings confirm the view that an employee-centered supervisor can achieve higher morale than a production-centered supervisor. Managers may well ask what is the relationship between this and production.

Supervision is production-oriented to the extent that it focuses attention on achieving organizational goals, and plans and devises methods for attaining them; it is employee-centered to the extent that it focuses attention on employee attitudes toward those goals, and plans and works toward maintenance of employee satisfaction.

High productivity and low morale result when a supervisor plans and organizes work efficiently but cannot achieve high membership satisfaction. Low production and high morale result when a supervisor, though keeping members satisfied with his leadership, either has not gained acceptance of organizational goals or does not have the technical competence to achieve them.

The relationship between supervision, morale, and productivity is an interdependent one, with the supervisor playing an integral role due to his ability to influence productivity and morale independently of each other.

A supervisor who can plan his work well has good technical knowledge, and who can install better production methods can raise production without necessarily increasing group satisfaction. On the other hand, a supervisor who can motivate his employees and keep them satisfied with his leadership can gain high production in spite of technical difficulties and environmental obstacles.

CLIMATE AND SUPERVISION

Climate, the intangible environment of an organization made up of attitudes, beliefs, and traditions, plays a large part in morale, productivity, and supervision. Usually when we speak of climate and its relationship to morale and productivity, we talk about the merits of *democratic* versus *authoritarian* climate. Employees seem to produce more and have higher morale in a democratic climate, whereas in an authoritarian climate, the reverse seems to be true or so the researchers tell us. We would do well to determine what these terms mean to supervision.

Perhaps most of our difficulty in understanding and applying these concepts comes from our emotional reactions to the words themselves. For example, authoritarian climate is usually painted as the very blackest kind of dictatorship. This is not surprising, because we are usually expected to believe that it is invariably bad. Conversely, democratic climate is drawn to make the driven snow look impure by comparison.

Now these descriptions are most probably true when we talk about our political processes, or town meetings, or freedom of speech. However, the same labels have been used by social scientists in other contexts and have also been applied to government and business organizations, without it, it seems, any recognition that the meanings and their social values may have changed somewhat

For example, these labels were used in experiments conducted in an informal classroom setting using 11-year-old boys as subjects. The descriptive labels applied to the climate of the setting as well as the type of leadership practiced. When these labels were transferred to a management setting, it seems that many presumed that they principally meant the king of leadership rather than climate. We can see that there is a great difference between the experimental and management settings and that leadership practices for one might be inappropriate for the other.

It is doubtful that formal work organizations can be anything but authoritarian, in that goals are set by management and a hierarchy exists through which decisions and orders from the top are transmitted downward. Organizations are authoritarian by structure and need; direction and control are placed in the hands of a few in order to gain fast and efficient decision making. Now this does not mean to describe a dictatorship. It is merely the recognition of the fact that direction of organizational affairs comes from above. It should be noted that leadership in some natural groups is, in this sense, authoritarian.

Granting that formal organizations have this kind of authoritarian leadership, can there be a democratic climate? Certainly there can be, but we would want to define and delimit this term. A more realistic meaning of democratic climate in organizations is the use of permissive and participatory methods in management-employee relations. That is, a mutual exchange of information and explanation with the granting of individual freedom within certain restricted and defined limits. However, it is not our purpose to debate the merits of authoritarianism versus democracy. We recognize that within the small work group there is a need for freedom from constraint and an increase in participation in order to achieve organizational goals within the framework of the organizational movement.

Another aspect of climate is best expressed by this familiar, and true, saying: actions speak louder than words. Of particular concern to us is this effect of management climate on the behavior of supervisors, particularly in employee-centered activities.

There have been reports of disappointment with efforts to make supervisors ore employee-centered. Managers state that, since research has shown ways of improving human relations, supervisors should begin to practice these methods. Usually a training course in human relations is established; and supervisors are given this training. Managers then sit back and wait for the expected improvements, only to find that there are none.

If we wish to produce changes in the supervisor's behavior, the climate must be made appropriate and rewarding to the changed behavior. This means that top-level attitudes and behavior cannot deny or contradict the change we are attempting to effect. Basic changes in organizational behavior cannot be made with any permanence, unless we provide an environment that is receptive to the changes and rewards those persons who do change.

IMPROVING SUPERVISION

Anyone who has read this far might expect to find *A Dozen Rules for Dealing With Employees* or *29 Steps to Supervisory Success*. We will not provide such a list.

Simple rules suffer from their simplicity. They ignore the complexities of human behavior. Reliance upon rules may cause supervisors to concentrate on superficial aspects of their relations with employees. It may preclude genuine understanding.

The supervisor who relies on a list of rules tends to think of people in mechanistic terms. In a certain situation, he uses *Rule No. 3*. Employees are not treated as thinking and feeling persons, but rather as figures in a formula: Rule 3 applied to employee X = Production.

Employees usually recognize mechanical manipulation and become dissatisfied and resentful. They lose faith in, and respect for, their supervisor, and this may be reflected in lower morale and productivity.

We do not mean that supervisors must become social science experts if they wish to improve. Reports of current research indicate that there are two major parts of their job which can be strengthened through self-improvement: (1) Work planning, including technical skills, and (2) motivation of employees.

The most effective supervisors combine excellence in the administrative and technical aspects of their work with friendly and considerate personal relations with their employees.

13

CRITICAL PERSONAL RELATIONS

Later in this chapter we shall talk about administrative aspects of supervision, but first let us comment on *friendly and considerate personal relations*. We have discussed this subject throughout the preceding chapters, but we want to review some of the critical supervisory influences on personal relations.

Closeness of Supervision: The closeness of supervision has an important effect on productivity and morale. Mann and Dent found that supervisors of low-producing units supervise very closely, while high-producing supervisors exercise only general supervision. It was found that the low-producing supervisors:

- check on employees more frequently
- give more detailed and frequent instructions
- limit employee's freedom to do job in own way

Workers who felt less closely supervised reported that they were better satisfied with their jobs and the company. We should note that the manner or attitude of the supervisor has an important bearing on whether employees perceive supervision as being close or general.

These findings are another way of saying that supervision does not mean standing over the employee and telling him what to do and when and how to do it. The more effective supervisor tells his employees what is required, giving general instructions.

COMMUNICATION

Supervisors of high-production units consider communication as one of the most important aspects of their job. Effective communication is used by these supervisors to achieve better interpersonal relations and improved employee motivation. Low-production supervisors do not rate communications as highly important.

High-producing supervisors find that an important aid to more effective communication is listening. They are ready to listen to both personal problems or interests and questions about the work. This does not mean that they are *nosey* or meddle in their employees' personal lives, but rather that they show a willingness to listen, and do listen, if their employees wish to discuss problems.

These supervisors inform employees about forthcoming changes in work; they discuss agency policy with employees; and they make sure that each employee knows how well he is doing. What these supervisors do is use two-way communication effectively. Unless the supervisor freely imparts information, he will not receive information in return.

Attitudes and perception are frequently affected by communication or the lack of it. Research surveys reveal that many supervisors are not aware of their employees' attitudes, nor do they know what personal reactions their supervision arouses. Through frank discussion with employees, they have been surprised to discover employee beliefs about which they were ignorant. Discussion sometimes reveals that the supervisor and his employees have totally different impressions about the same event. The supervisor should be constantly on the alert for misconceptions about his words and deeds. He must remember that, although his actions are perfectly clear to himself, they may be, and frequently are, viewed differently by employees.

Failure to communicate information results in misconceptions and false assumptions. What you say and how you say it will strongly affect your employees' attitudes and perceptions. By giving them available information, you can prevent misconceptions; by discussion, you may be able to change attitudes; by questioning, you can discover what the perceptions and assumptions really are. And it need hardly be added that actions should conform very closely to words.

If we were to attempt to reduce the above discussion on communication to rules, we would have a long list which would be based on one cardinal principle: Don't make assumptions!

- Don't assume that your employees know; tell them.
- Don't assume that you know how they feel; find out.
- Don't assume that they understand; clarify.

20 SUPERVISORY HINTS

1. Avoid inconsistency.
2. Always give employees a chance to explain their action before taking disciplinary action. Don't allow too much time for a "cooling off" period before disciplining an employee.
3. Be specific in your criticisms.
4. Delegate responsibility wisely.
5. Do not argue or lose your temper, and avoid being impatient.
6. Promote mutual respect and be fair, impartial, and open-minded.
7. Keep in mind that asking for employees' advice and input can be helpful in decision making.
8. If you make promises, keep them.
9. Always keep the feelings, abilities, dignity and motives of your staff in mind.
10. Remain loyal to your employees' interests.
11. Never criticize employees in front of others, or treat employees like children.
12. Admit mistakes. Don't place blame on your employees, or make excuses.
13. Be reasonable in your expectations, give complete instructions, and establish well-planned goals.
14. Be knowledgeable about office details and procedures, but avoid becoming bogged down in details.
15. Avoid supervising too closely or too loosely. Employees should also view you as an approachable supervisor.
16. Remember that employees' personal problems may affect job performance, but become involved only when appropriate.
17. Work to develop workers, and to instill a feeling of cooperation while working toward mutual goals.
18. Do not overpraise or underpraise, be properly appreciative.
19. Never ask an employee to discipline someone for you.
20. A complaint, even if unjustified, should be taken seriously.

16

NOTES

www.ingramcontent.com/pod-product-compliance
Lightning Source LLC
Chambersburg PA
CBHW082207300426
44117CB00016B/2696